THE UPPER ROOM

DAILY MEDITATIONS FROM AROUND THE WORLD

Stephen D. Bryant
Editor and Publisher

INTERDENOMINATIONAL
INTERNATIONAL
INTERRACIAL

77 EDITIONS
40 LANGUAGES

The Upper Room
July–December 2009
Edited by Susan Hibbins

The Upper Room © BRF 2009
The Bible Reading Fellowship
15 The Chambers, Vineyard, Abingdon OX14 3FE
Tel: 01865 319700; Fax: 01865 319701
Email: enquiries@brf.org.uk
Website: www.brf.org.uk
ISBN 978 1 84101 751 8

Acknowledgments

The New Revised Standard Version of the Bible, Anglicized Edition, copyright © 1989, 1995 by the Division of Christian Education of the National Council of the Churches of Christ in the USA. Used by permission. All rights reserved.

The Holy Bible, New International Version, copyright © 1973, 1978, 1984 by International Bible Society. Used by permission of Hodder & Stoughton Publishers, a division of Hodder Headline Ltd. All rights reserved. 'NIV' is a registered trademark of International Bible Society. UK trademark number 1448790.

Extracts from the Authorised Version of the Bible (The King James Bible), the rights in which are vested in the Crown, are reproduced by permission of the Crown's Patentee, Cambridge University Press.

Scriptures quoted from the Good News Bible published by The Bible Societies/HarperCollins Publishers Ltd, UK © American Bible Society 1966, 1971, 1976, 1992, used by permission.

Printed in the UK by HSW Print

Introducing BRF

We at The Bible Reading Fellowship (BRF) are delighted to become the publishers of the UK edition of The Upper Room. We have had a long association with The Upper Room's US publisher and have collaborated on a number of books over the years. We're very pleased also that Susan Hibbins has agreed to continue as Editor of this UK edition.

Who are BRF? We're a Christian Registered Charity, based in Abingdon, with a staff team of 25. We've been publishing Bible reading notes without interruption since January 1922, but there's a great deal more to BRF than just publishing devotionals! At the heart of our ministry is a desire to equip people for Christian living. This involves three strands — helping people to read and understand the Bible, helping them to explore prayer and helping them to grow as disciples of Jesus Christ. Through all that we do — producing resources, providing training, working face-to-face with adults and children, and via the web — we work to resource individuals and church communities in their Christian discipleship. (For more information about BRF visit our website www.brf.org.uk.)

Barnabas is the name under which we work with primary schools and churches throughout the UK. Under the strapline 'exploring Christianity creatively' we aim to equip adults working with children under the age of 11 to be more effective in their teaching, and to bring the Bible and Christian faith alive for the children themselves.

The Upper Room complements the other Bible reading notes series, New Daylight, Guidelines and Day by Day with God, that we already publish, enabling us to offer an even wider range of daily devotional resources within the UK. We want to encourage as many people as we can to read and reflect on God's word as a natural part of their daily lives.

Although this year The Upper Room has been published six-monthly, from January 2010 we will move to a four-monthly publishing cycle, in line with our other series. The three issues will be January-April, May-August and September-December (see page 213 for details of subscription rates for next year).

We hope you will enjoy this issue of The Upper Room and that you will help us to introduce it to others and inspire them to start reading it themselves.

Richard Fisher
Chief Executive

A Prayer of Presence

I like Tilden Edwards' simple description of prayer: 'Authentic prayer is opening to God's gracious presence with all that we are, with what scripture summarises as our whole heart, soul, and mind' (Matt. 22:37).[1] The quality of our prayer, then, depends on the quality — the honesty, and constancy — of our presence to God, not God's presence to us. After all, the problem that prayer addresses is not God's absence from us but our absence from God. The good news of God's grace is 'Emmanuel': God with us! And yet, we are elsewhere. We fall fast asleep, spiritually speaking; we forget our connectedness to God; we become lost in our sense of separateness and self-sufficiency.

So how do we cultivate the quality of our presence to God? I find benefit in a 'prayer of presence', a verse of adoration and praise that can keep us constantly alert to the wonder of God's presence radiating into daily life. My 'prayer of presence' comes from 'A Liturgy for Morning Prayer' in the *Upper Room Worshipbook*:

New every morning is your love, great God of light,
and all day long you are working for good in the world...[2]

As far as I am able, I keep this prayer in my heart as I walk to and from work and as I go about my daily routine. Do I do this to impress God or because God needs it to reach me? Not in the least. I pray this way because I need it, lest I forget God altogether. Some people fear that prayer of this kind will make them 'too heavenly minded to be of any earthly good'. But I have found that the effect is just the opposite: this prayer moves me to a richer awareness of life around me and within me, a greater readiness to respond to the promptings of divine love. May this issue's readings stir in you a desire for richer life with God.

Stephen D. Bryant
Editor and Publisher

Notes
1. Tilden Edwards, *Living in the Presence: Disciplines for the Spiritual Heart* (Harper and Row, 1987), p. 11.
2. *Upper Room Worshipbook* (Upper Room Books, 2006), p. 6.

The Editor writes...

I was once with a group of work colleagues, several of whom were known to be hostile to religion in general and Christianity in particular. We had just finished a company dinner, and conversation turned, as it sometimes does on these occasions, to 'the meaning of life'. Our boss challenged us to make a definition using only two sentences. After one or two people had made some rather cynical attempts, a member of staff, known to be a somewhat serious, churchgoing young man, said hesitantly, 'I can give you the meaning of life in two sentences: "You shall love the Lord your God with all your heart, and with all your soul, and with all your mind. And you shall love your neighbour as yourself."'

He flushed to the roots of his hair, and there was a dead silence round the table, but I fancied I could hear great cheers ringing out in heaven. For Jesus' words tell us in a nutshell what is, or should be, at the heart of our Christian faith. They are simple words, not so simple to live by, certainly, but they strip away all the unnecessary complications that take us away from what Jesus came to show us: a life of loving obedience that shows the same love to our neighbour.

Love cannot be forced; we love where and whom we want to, and in our best moments of feeling especially close to him, we yearn to love Jesus with our whole being, to become the people he wants us to be. But gazing at Jesus is not enough. It is as our friend that he asks us to turn outwards and gaze with that same love at each other. As you read and reflect on this issue of The Upper Room I pray you will be challenged and encouraged to do just that.

Susan Hibbins
Editor of the UK edition

P.S. I would like to add how pleased I am that BRF has now become the publisher of The Upper Room in the UK, and that I am to continue as Editor of the new edition. I shall look forward once again to receiving your meditations.

To contact me, write to me at BRF, 15 The Chambers, Vineyard, Abingdon OX14 3FE.

What We Need

Read Psalm 116:1-19*

[The LORD] put a new song in my mouth, a hymn of praise to our God.
Psalm 40:3 (NIV)

When I was diagnosed with a rare type of ovarian cancer, I spent hours researching my diagnosis on the Internet before I met with my oncologist. At our meeting I scribbled copious notes about the cancer, the chemotherapy, the chances of recurrence. But that information gave me no peace. While I feared chemotherapy, the possibility of recurrence paralysed me. Sadness began to invade even the happiest occasions of my life.

Answering my prayers for healing, God sent me a host of angels: cancer patients more seriously ill than I was witnessed to their faith through joyful living. Friends and family prayed for me. Books written by Christians with cancer addressed my fears. The psalmists comforted me, and Bible heroes — Daniel, Peter, Stephen, Paul — inspired me. I began to experience Christ, the greatest hero of all, walking with empathy beside me, healing me.

My treatment is finished, and today I feel wonderfully alive. I prayed for my deepest desire: a sure physical cure. Instead, Christ healed my spirit, replacing doubt and fear with trust and peace.

Prayer: *Dearest Lord, thank you for bringing us wholeness and, sometimes, physical healing. Thank you for your faithful angels who witness to the possibility of joy in life's most difficult times. Amen.*

Thought for the Day: 'Whether we live or die, we belong to the Lord' (Rom. 14:8, NIV).

Lottie Guttry (Texas)

* The Bible readings are selected with great care, and we urge you to include the suggested reading in your devotional time.

Called by Name

Read John 10:1-15
The sheep hear [the shepherd's] voice. He calls his own sheep by name and leads them out. John 10:3 (NRSV)

I loved visiting the farm where my uncle raised goats. In the evening about milking time, the cheerful lights of the barn were turned on and the goats would line up at the door. This was a special moment of the day when each goat received special attention from my uncle. He would call a name, and one by one the goats got on the milking stand. Here they were relieved of their heavy burden of milk.

My uncle spoke to each goat as he milked her. His muscular hands stroked them, and he examined each one for any cuts or bruises. When this process was over, each goat would jump down and go to her own stall where supper was waiting. They were well cared for.

God knows that we too need attention. We are included in God's flock. How wonderful that God cares deeply and personally about each one of us! Our Creator knows us and calls us by name.

Prayer: *Thank you, God, for calling us by name and giving us your personal attention. Accept our humble gratitude, through Christ our shepherd and Lord as we pray, 'Father, hallowed be your name, your kingdom come. Give us each day our daily bread. Forgive us our sins, for we also forgive everyone who sins against us. And lead us not into temptation.'* Amen.*

Thought for the Day: God calls each one of us by name.

John W. McKinstry (Massachusetts)

Thank-o-meter

Read Psalm 30
O LORD my God, I will give you thanks forever. Psalm 30:12 (NIV)

Not long ago I bought a pedometer — one of those gizmos to clip onto my waistband to measure how many steps I take. I read somewhere that we should take at least ten thousand steps a day to stay healthy.

One day a friend told me she wondered what score she would have if, instead of a pedometer, she wore a 'thank-o-meter' — a little machine to measure how much gratitude we have, instead of how far we walk.

Learning to be grateful, no matter what our circumstances are, is always important. We have much to say thank you for, but often we're too busy or don't notice the good that is around us. Most of us have more blessings than we can count. But even if everything were stripped away, I would still have the love of God and the hope that comes from knowing Jesus Christ as my Saviour. Realising that I have God's grace and salvation for all eternity — now that calls for giving thanks.

Prayer: *Father God, how can we ever thank you for all you have done for us? Show us how we can live with thankfulness in our hearts and how that gratitude can spill over and touch others around us. Amen.*

Thought for the Day: How many blessings can I count today?

Bryony Wood (Nottinghamshire, England)

How Would Jesus Play?

Read Matthew 24:45-47
Lead a life worthy of the calling to which you have been called.
Ephesians 4:1 (NRSV)

It's not whether you win or lose, it's how you play the game. One of the officials who was scheduled to attend our daughter's high-school basketball game failed to arrive. The host school offered to forfeit the game, but our team declined the offer, opting to play anyway.

The lone official explained to the girls that he would be unable to see everything and that he would need their help. As the game progressed, we observed the true spirit of athletic competition. When the referee was unable to see, the girls responded by admitting violations. When a call was in doubt, the offending player acknowledged that she had committed the foul or was out of bounds. That evening the focus was clearly on how they played the game.

These high-school girls served as an example for us all as we face daily decisions. We must make the call: reporting or not reporting undocumented income; being faithful or unfaithful to our spouse; engaging or not engaging in hurtful gossip. Do we live honestly even when telling the truth brings consequences we would like to avoid?

On a spiritual level, we decide whether to take part in the ministries of the church and whether to forgive those who have done us wrong. As we monitor our own lives, do we live according to the Bible?

Prayer: *Dear God, give us courage to be faithful to Christ in our daily actions. Amen.*

Thought for the Day: Every choice offers an opportunity to follow Christ.

Roy Shaver (Missouri)

God Under Fire

Read Psalm 56 and Deuteronomy 20:1-4
In the shadow of your wings [O God] I will take refuge, until the destroying storms pass by. Psalm 57:1 (NRSV)

I picked up the magazine, eager to be inspired by its cover story about military chaplains striving to live the word of God under fire in Iraq. To my dismay, the article began with the story of one young chaplain whose faith had been so shattered by what he saw in war that he wanted nothing to do with God, who had become sick of religion and had come to hate God.

It hurt me to read this account about faith in crisis. But I had to ask myself: What would it take to turn me away from God? A bitter divorce? The death of one of my children? Incurable cancer? I understood that chaplain whose inner struggles had caused him to become bitter, angry and alienated.

I read on to discover that the man in question, now counselling wounded military personnel at a government hospital, had recovered his faith. After agonising months of adjustment back at home, he found and described a new relationship with God brought about by what he had experienced. After enduring a difficult time that challenged his beliefs and changed his life, this soldier/pastor returned to God, a different person but still a believer.

As his story showed me, times of doubt can become a doorway to renewed faith.

Prayer: *Lord Jesus, take whatever faith we have and make it grow, day by day. Amen.*

Thought for the Day: On the other side of doubt and struggle is a door into deeper faith.

Prudence Schofield (Maine)

The Holy Spirit

Read Mark 1:4-8

Hope does not disappoint us, because God's love has been poured into our hearts through the Holy Spirit that has been given to us.
Romans 5:5 (NRSV)

As I listened to the pastor's message, her words caught my attention. She was saying that she wished everyone to receive the baptism of the Holy Spirit. I thought, I am a Christian. I have already been baptised. Why does she talk about being baptised again? I was confused.

Then our church held a special evangelistic meeting. We invited a guest preacher for the meeting, and I wondered if he would help me with my doubt and questions. During the meeting, the preacher invited people to come forward; but I didn't go because I was disappointed in his preaching. My questions about the Holy Spirit had not been answered.

The next evening, I attended church again. The pastor asked people to pray longer than usual. All the people prayed together. To my great surprise, the pastor came to me while I was praying and put her hand on my shoulder. As she prayed for me, I felt the love of God deeply. In that moment, I realised that the Holy Spirit was already within me. My eyes filled with tears of joy.

Prayer: *Loving God, help us to know you more fully. By the power of the Holy Spirit, fill us with your love. Amen.*

Thought for the Day: How do I recognise the Holy Spirit within me?

Kazumi Munehiro (Fukuoka, Japan)

Eyes of Love

Read Psalm 103:1-12
The LORD is compassionate and gracious, slow to anger, abounding in love. Psalm 103:8 (NIV)

I am an optimist; I assume the best of people. In fact, I see the bright side so often that I'm accused of wearing rose-coloured glasses. It isn't true that looking at the world positively is a way to avoid facing reality. I am very realistic; I know evil exists. But I try to filter my view through the eyes of love.

Does this attitude set me up for pain and disappointment? Sometimes. However, I believe God looks at me through rose-coloured glasses; God continually gives me the benefit of the doubt. God knows my mean thoughts, jealous tendencies and lazy attitudes. God sees me yell at my son, lose patience at work, snap at my husband, and show indifference to the needy. In spite of my misdeeds, God looks at me with eyes of love. God is not blind to our sins but forgives us when we ask. As I view the world and its great potential, my attitude enables me to look with greater compassion. Following God's example, I find it easier to forgive the hurts when they come.

Prayer: *Dear Father, thank you for looking at us with love and compassion and for forgiving our sins. Today, help us to see others with that same love and to forgive as we have been forgiven. Amen.*

Thought for the Day: Look at the world with the eyes of love.

Lisa Bogart (California)

12 **PRAYER FOCUS:** TO SEE AND AFFIRM THE BEST IN PEOPLE

Spiritual Balance

Read Isaiah 40:28-31

Because so many people were coming and going that [the apostles] did not even have a chance to eat, [Jesus] said to them, 'Come with me by yourselves to a quiet place and get some rest.' Mark 6:31 (NIV)

In retirement I found myself becoming a full-time volunteer. While volunteering is personally rewarding, at times it can also lead to stress and frustration. One day a friend shared her concern that I was doing too much. It gave me pause for reflection. Why am I volunteering? Is it because I can't say 'No'? Or is it something deeper inside, such as the need to be needed and noticed? Have I been serving just to receive the affirmation of others?

I've since learned to do less and to spend more time in prayer and reflection. In neglecting my inner being, I was becoming spiritually unbalanced. In serving and doing for others, I wasn't waiting on the Lord for strength and direction. I'd forgotten what Jesus said: 'Apart from me you can do nothing' (John 15:5).

No one was more pressed into doing things for others than Jesus. The crowds gave him no relief. So it was necessary — even for Jesus — to draw apart and pray for strength and wisdom in serving others. Should we seek anything less?

Prayer: *O God, remind us every day to rest and renew our spirits in you. Amen.*

Thought for the Day: To be an effective volunteer, I need spiritual balance.

Donald Joiner (North Carolina)

My Hope

Read 1 Peter 5:6-10

May our Lord Jesus Christ himself, and God our Father, who loved us and through grace gave us eternal comfort and good hope, comfort your hearts. 2 Thessalonians 2:16-17 (NRSV)

My life has been filled with hard trials. When I was just two or three days old, I almost died because of the midwife's carelessness. Ever since then, I have suffered from various illnesses. Then, when I was a teenager, I had a kidney operation that left me unable to have children.

When I got married, I decided to adopt a child, Iva. Although I loved her unconditionally, I was very upset because she too was ill. I struggled alone with her illnesses, without the support of my husband, an alcoholic. While I was taking care of Iva, my mother-in-law tried to take her away from me. Eventually, Iva died in my arms at the age of 13. I felt absolutely helpless but managed to find strength for the next trial — my husband divorcing me.

I wouldn't be alive now if I didn't know Christ. Fortunately, during all those long years of suffering, I was a Christian. When my daughter died and I couldn't see a direction in my life, God showed me the right way and gave me a message of comfort, just as Hagar was comforted in the desert. Through my struggles I learned an important lesson: we cannot blame God when we suffer. We live in a sinful world filled with imperfect people, but God is perfect and merciful. God is our hope.

Prayer: *God of all compassion, help us to feel your presence and comfort in times of suffering. Amen.*

Thought for the Day: Everyone suffers, but believers never have to suffer alone.

Anna Georgieva (Pleven, Bulgaria)

Surprising Mercy

Read Jonah 3-4

The LORD said, 'Nineveh has more than a hundred and twenty thousand people who cannot tell their right hand from their left… Should I not be concerned about that great city?' Jonah 4:11 (NIV)

God told Jonah to proclaim the destruction of Nineveh, Assyria's capital city. When Jonah preached this message, all of Nineveh fasted, wore sackcloth, and prayed. 'Who knows?' spoke the king, 'Maybe God will show mercy.' Hearing of their repentance and God's mercy extended, Jonah became angry because he wanted God's harsh judgement to fall on the Ninevites.

When people hear that I am Assyrian, some ask, 'Like in the Bible?' Indeed, yes! In ancient times, the Assyrians delighted in terrorising other kingdoms, especially Israel. God did eventually judge Assyria but still spared the people. Though the empire fell around 625 BC, today we Assyrians are thousands strong — scattered around the world — among the first nations to accept the gospel and still worshippers of Christ. Because of this, we have endured countless persecutions throughout the centuries. Assyrians living in the Middle East today are still persecuted for following Christ and not Islam or other religions. We Assyrians can thank God for pushing Jonah to overcome his judgement of the Ninevites and warn them.

Is there anyone in our lives that we, like Jonah, want God to condemn? Instead, to our shock, God asks us to love them, to show grace and mercy, setting aside our feelings. Who knows? Maybe our obedient love is the very thing God will use to help someone find life in Christ.

Prayer: *Lord, help us to love those we find hard to love. May we work together to spread your love all over the world. Amen.*

Thought for the Day: God's love — working through us — can save the world.

Sabrina Savra (Illinois)

Getting to Know You

Read John 15:12-17

Jesus said, 'If you really knew me, you would know my Father as well. From now on, you do know him and have seen him.' John 14:7 (NIV)

I looked forward to a forthcoming writers' conference, but I wondered about the woman I had requested as a roommate. She was an acquaintance, someone I had met through our writers' group; but I didn't know her well. Would we get on? Would we become friends?

As it turned out, we did enjoy each other's company. As the week progressed, we spent a lot of time together. Through long talks full of personal stories, encouraging words and laughter, we got to know each other on a deeper level. My roommate and I started the week as acquaintances, but we ended the week as dear friends.

We become friends with Christ in a similar manner. In John 15:15, Jesus says, 'I no longer call you servants... Instead, I have called you friends.' Focusing on Jesus, reading his words, and listening for his guidance brings us into a committed, loving relationship with our Saviour.

Prayer: *Lord Jesus Christ, we want to know you and love you. Help us make the effort to sustain lasting friendship with you. Amen.*

Thought for the Day: Is Christ a good friend or merely a convenient acquaintance?

Angie Kay Dilmore (Louisiana)

Not What is Easy

Read Hebrews 13:1-8

We can say with confidence, 'The Lord is my helper; I will not be afraid. What can anyone do to me?' Hebrews 13:6 (NRSV)

When my father-in-law, Bob Alexander, was a young man he was proud of his lean and wiry physique. Bob enjoyed hard physical work and was well known for his strength. He was also a minister. His strong sense of God's desire for justice caused him to fight hard for the dignity and rights of the underprivileged in the churches he served.

In the late 1950s, along with other courageous clergy, Bob took a stand against racial segregation, not only in the community but also in his church. He was tough, confident of what God wanted, and in the right. Nevertheless, Bob's young family was threatened; his job was at risk; a cross was burned in protest of his work. His reputation for being able to lift the front end of a truck could not help him in this situation.

Bob's actions highlight a difficult truth: God calls us to do what is right, not what is easy. Yet my father-in-law was able to allow himself not to be controlled by worry because he knew that the Lord was his helper. The opponents did not disappear, but the Lord gave Bob and his family confidence and peace. No threat then or now has the power to separate any Jesus-follower from the healing love of our faithful God.

Prayer: *Dear God, give us the courage to stand up for the rights of all people, trusting that you will stand with us. Amen.*

Thought for the Day: Even life's most frightening moments cannot separate us from the love of God.

Derek Maul (Florida)

Persistent in Prayer

Read Luke 11:5-13

Jesus said, 'I tell you, though he will not get up and give him the bread because he is his friend, yet because of the man's boldness he will get up and give him as much as he needs.' Luke 11:8 (NIV)

While my friend and I were on holiday, we often went to sit by the lake while we ate lunch. One day as we sat eating our sandwiches, a family and their lovely black Labrador retriever appeared. They had come to enjoy the beauty of the lake too. Their dog found a stick and then made it very clear that he wanted it thrown into the lake so he could fetch it and have a swim at the same time. The dog kept following the man and placing the stick at his feet. Then the dog would run back and forth between the man and the lake. When that did not work, the dog stood on his back legs and gently placed his front paws on the man's legs. In desperation, the dog began to bark, and finally his master responded. Boldness and persistence worked.

As the scripture passage tells us, boldness also works in human relationships. The persistent friend finally gets what he needs. Watching the dog's persistence and boldness that afternoon made me think: Should I not be just as persistent and bold when praying for friends and family? Luke 11:9 says, 'Knock and the door will be opened to you.' The model that scripture offers is to be persistent and bold in our praying.

Prayer: *Dear Father God, help us to keep praying and to keep reaching out in love to those around us. Amen.*

Thought for the Day: Never, never, never give up. Keep praying.

Janet Walker (Buckinghamshire, England)

They Also Serve

Read Exodus 4:10-16

Moses said unto the LORD, O my Lord, I am not eloquent, neither heretofore, nor since thou hast spoken unto thy servant: but I am slow of speech, and of a slow tongue. Exodus 4:10 (KJV)

God would not allow Moses to use a handicap as an excuse to back away from what God asked him to do. After Moses had reluctantly agreed, he found that with God's guidance, he was able to lead the people out of bondage.

Through the ages, God has strengthened and worked through those with impairments. Their accomplishments have been a witness to what is possible when we realise that God is with us. Both John Milton, the British poet who, though blind, wrote *Paradise Lost*, and speaker and writer Helen Keller, who was both deaf and blind, are awesome examples of the power of God. When we have an emptiness, God fills it.

When I become despondent because of the physical impairments of my advancing years, I remember the nation that grew from Abraham and Sarah, who seemed too old to have a child. If I give myself to my church and community, God will still work through me. In whatever I do, I can serve as a witness that God will use my gifts and talents, despite the limitations that come with ageing.

Prayer: *O Lord, help us find opportunities to help others. Amen.*

Thought for the Day: At every stage of our lives, God can use our talents to serve others.

Raymond Bottom (Mississippi)

PRAYER FOCUS: THOSE ADJUSTING TO PHYSICAL LIMITATIONS

Hidden Fruit

Read Psalm 119:7-20

All scripture is inspired by God and is useful for teaching, for reproof, for correction, and for training in righteousness, so that everyone who belongs to God may be proficient, equipped for every good work.
2 Timothy 3:16-17 (NRSV)

One of my favourite summer activities is picking wild raspberries. I love to stand in one spot and to pick as many raspberries as I can find (hopefully, enough for a pie!) before moving on to the next patch. Often when I think I have exhausted the supply of berries before me, I prepare to move on, only to spy the ripest, biggest, most luscious berry yet. How did I miss this one? I wonder. The answer is simple: changing my stance and my line of sight lets me see what had been there all along, waiting for me to claim it.

In a way, the same is true with God's word. At times I become complacent, even bored, with a passage of scripture, thinking I have exhausted its meaning and relevance to my life. When time and experience have changed my outlook on life, however, I find myself re-reading the passage and thinking, How did I miss that? Surprised I didn't see some message sooner, but grateful to have the newfound insight, I am enriched. Yes, the wisdom is fresh and new every morning (see Lam. 3:23). Thanks be to God!

Prayer: *Dear God, thank you for the Bible and all the riches it contains. Help us to go on learning from it as long as we live. In Jesus' name we pray. Amen.*

Thought for the Day: What new insights can I gather from the Bible today?

Kristine Liknes (Ohio)

'Don't Be Afraid'

Read Mark 6:45-51
Jesus said, 'Take courage! It is I. Don't be afraid.' Mark 6:50 (NIV)

To me, the world is a frightening place. The police claim that crime is falling, but it isn't from what I can see. It seems that just when I begin to feel safe, there are new acts of terrorism. Health and financial issues are constant worries, and to top it off, we in Kansas face yearly threats of tornadoes.

In biblical times, people struggled with similar problems, including natural dangers. One such struggle occurred after Jesus left his disciples to go to the hills to pray alone. The disciples began struggling to cross the lake in the middle of a storm. While they were straining to row against the wind, Jesus came to them, walking on the water. When they cried out, thinking him a ghost, Jesus identified himself and told the disciples not to be afraid. As soon as Jesus entered the boat, the storm ended.

I need to hear these words, 'Don't be afraid' in my heart all the time. I find that only the grace, love, mercy and power of Christ can get me through times of fear. Feeling Christ's presence allows us to face life's frightening moments with the assurance that we are not alone. No matter what happens, we are eternally safe with Christ, who is our strength.

Prayer: *Life can be frightening, Lord. Be our strength. Speak the words, 'Don't be afraid' to quiet fearful hearts. Amen.*

Thought for the Day: Where do I see Christ in the middle of my storm?

Willard Stringham (Kansas)

My Ebenezer

Read 1 Samuel 7:2-12

Samuel took a stone and set it up between Mizpah and Shen. He named it Ebenezer, saying, 'Thus far has the LORD helped us.' 1 Samuel 7:12 (NIV)

My granddaughter was looking through an old hymnbook. She began reading aloud, 'Here I raise mine Ebenezer; hither by thy help I'm come.'* She stopped and asked, 'Grandma, what does Ebenezer mean?' Together, we discovered that an Ebenezer is a kind of memorial made of stones; it symbolises God's help and guidance.

My granddaughter and I talked together about things that remind us of God's love. We remembered the story of Jacob's dream and God's promise to bless him (see Gen. 28:10-22). Jacob poured oil over the stone he had used as a pillow and set it apart as a memorial of his encounter with God.

We read about Joshua leading the tribes of Israel across the Jordan River (see Josh. 4). A representative from each tribe carried a stone from the middle of the river, and Joshua set them up together as a permanent reminder of God's care.

We, too, can have 'Ebenezers'. It is good at times to look back — to how we came to know God, to healing, to answered prayers — and to remember that God who was mightily present at those times walks with us day by day as our guide and our help.

Prayer: *Thank you, Lord, that as we look back through our lives you remind us of the times we have experienced your loving care. Thank you for the assurance that your love never fails. Amen.*

Thought for the Day: Look back and see where you might set up your Ebenezers.

Elvie Klein (Queensland, Australia)

*Robert Robinson, 'Come, thou fount of every blessing'

New Creation

Read Isaiah 65:17-25

The LORD said, 'Behold, I will create new heavens and a new earth. The former things will not be remembered, nor will they come to mind. But be glad and rejoice forever in what I will create, for I will create Jerusalem to be a delight and its people a joy.' Isaiah 65:17-18 (NIV)

In anticipation of the forthcoming move from my home of 20 years, I carefully collected the seeds of my favourite plants from my beloved garden. After the move, I immediately planted the seeds in the garden of my new house. To my dismay, nothing came up — because the climate was different and not at all suitable for many of the southern plants whose seeds I had so carefully brought with me. I had moved nearly 700 miles north!

Instead of trying to recreate my old garden, I spent the first summer observing the plants that already flourished in the garden of my new home. Consequently, I was never without glorious blooms for my vases. I decided that the next spring I would create a new garden — one that was in harmony with the plants that were already established. My new garden would be different but in its own way just as lovely as the one I had left.

I came to see that I too would need to change, in order to adapt to my new community. I trusted God, the Master Gardener who creates us anew to thrive in whatever location we find ourselves, to nurture me through this challenging time.

Prayer: *Dear God, give us the wisdom and the patience to watch and wait for your new creation in our lives. Amen.*

Thought for the Day: Take delight in the new things God is doing in your life.

Sarah Schaller Linn (Wisconsin)

PRAYER FOCUS: THOSE MOVING TO A NEW HOME

Expecting the Best

Read Ephesians 3:14-21

Now unto [God] that is able to do exceeding abundantly above all that we ask or think, according to the power that worketh in us, unto him be glory. Ephesians 3:20-21 (KJV)

A few years back, I injured the rotator cuff in my shoulder. Suffering great pain, I decided to see an orthopaedic surgeon. He gave me a shot of steroids and prescribed physical therapy. Frankly, I was not expecting much relief. But to my surprise, within a few weeks the pain was virtually gone.

This led me to think about my spiritual life. Sometimes I pray, then pray again; but whether I pray about finances, relationships or peace of mind, I do not really expect the Lord to answer. So I decided to start praying expectantly. I did not imagine that God would say 'yes' to all of my prayers, but I prayed with a new attitude and new hope regarding God's response to my petitions. And I have not been disappointed.

Prayer: *Dear God, however you answer our prayers, let us be at peace with your response, knowing that you have our best interests in mind. As Jesus taught us, we pray, 'Our Father which art in heaven, Hallowed be thy name. Thy kingdom come. Thy will be done, as in heaven, so in earth. Give us day by day our daily bread. And forgive us our sins; for we also forgive every one that is indebted to us. And lead us not into temptation; but deliver us from evil.'* Amen.*

Thought for the Day: Sometimes the Lord grants us what we want as well as what we need.

Edward Sarp (Pennsylvania)

PRAYER FOCUS: THOSE RECOVERING FROM INJURIES
*Luke 11:2-4 (KJV)

God of the Universe

Read Psalm 8

When I look at your heavens, the work of your fingers, the moon and the stars that you have established; what are human beings that you are mindful of them, mortals that you care for them? Psalm 8:3-4 (NRSV)

'Do you ever think we'll put a man on the moon?' In my youth, the answer to that question was usually, 'I doubt it.' But 40 years ago I joined millions around the world who watched Neil Armstrong step onto the lunar surface. Not long ago I gazed into the heavens and watched a streak of light track across the night sky, light from a space station where astronauts orbit miles above the earth. Space is no longer beyond our reach.

The exploration of space has confirmed for us the vastness of our solar system and the universe beyond. I may never travel in space, and certainly I won't be able to reach its limits. Yet every day I can enjoy first-hand closeness with the omnipotent God who spoke all this into existence. The psalmist, who could only imagine what existed beyond the visible heavens, was certain about what existed in the heart of the God who created them: love and concern for humankind. And the psalmist was awed by the concept, as we should be.

Even if I were able to travel past the farthest star, I know that journey could never take me beyond the love and care of God. To me, that truth is more astounding than the vastness of space.

Prayer: *God of the limitless universe, thank you for the wonderful world you allow us to enjoy. Amen.*

Thought for the Day: God cares for every part of creation.

Richard L. Mabry (Texas)

Graceful Relating

Read Romans 12:4-18

The Sovereign LORD is my strength; he makes my feet like the feet of a deer, he enables me to go on the heights. Habakkuk 3:19 (NIV)

Recently I had a fright while riding my bicycle. I was racing along on a downhill slope when an adult deer darted out from the woods, on course for a collision with me. I swerved and tried to stop, but an accident seemed imminent. To my relief, the deer turned, ran alongside me, and then gracefully dashed back into the woods. Her movements seemed effortless; the whole incident took only seconds. One moment I feared I'd be jolted off my bicycle and badly hurt. The next, I was peering into the woods looking for the gentle creature. I thanked God that I was safe and watched out for deer on the rest of my ride.

Later, as I reflected on the damage a collision might have caused, I thought about God's call for us to be peacemakers. In Romans 12:18 Paul wrote, 'If it is possible, as far as it depends on you, live at peace with everyone' (NIV). This call gives me hope to grow in my ability to respond gently to others and to turn away from causing them harm. In this way, I'm doing my part to live peacefully with others.

With our words or actions, we can either cause collisions or gracefully avoid hurting others. The encounter with that doe encourages me to think of God's power making 'my feet like the feet of a deer', enabling me to avoid hurting those around me.

Prayer: *O God, help us to make peace and to deal graciously with others. Amen.*

Thought for the Day: The way we treat others matters to God.

Linda Walstrom (Illinois)

Praying Always

Read Ephesians 6:10-20
Pray in the Spirit at all times in every prayer and supplication.
Ephesians 6:18 (NRSV)

In the middle of a busy city, my wife and I waited to cross the road. I pressed the button for the pedestrian crossing sign once, twice, half a dozen times.

'Why did you do that?' asked my wife. 'Once is enough. You are not going to speed anything up by doing it again and again.'

'I know,' I replied, 'but it makes me feel better.'

Her question made me think of one of my own 'whys'. The Bible encourages us to pray with confidence, knowing that our requests are heard. But it also tells us to pray constantly. I have wondered why, but I have concluded that prayer is so much in the realm of mystery that I cannot expect to understand. Nevertheless I try.

Prayer is as much for me as it is for God. Though I would like to think that the world is different because I pray, I know that all I can do is to rely on God and simply pray in faith. But regardless of what happens in the world outside me, when I pray, something happens within me. Not only do I feel better, but I am also changed by the experience. Sometimes I don't want to pray about a problem that is troubling me, and I resist. When I pray, God sorts out my motives. Then the world seems different because I am different, and I am more confident in leaving the final answers to God.

Prayer: *Come, Lord Jesus. Inspire us by your presence. Amen.*

Thought for the Day: Prayer helps us to see ourselves and our motives more honestly.

Bill Adams (Queensland, Australia)

Player or Spectator?

Read 1 Samuel 3:1-10

I heard the voice of the LORD saying, 'Whom shall I send? And who will go for us?' And I said, 'Here am I. Send me!' Isaiah 6:8 (NIV)

Years ago I attended the funeral of Ralph Callahan, a man who at the age of 93 had been the oldest working journalist in my state, Alabama. Because of his senior status, Ralph liked to say that he had a 'licence to reminisce'. He was especially grateful to still be involved in a profession that he loved. The minister at the funeral talked about Ralph's zest for living, saying that life for Ralph was never a spectator sport. He was a player.

When I joined my church, I asked myself, Will I be a player or a spectator? 'Here am I. Send me', we read in Isaiah. But saying yes to a call to discipleship can be hard, especially if it takes us out of our comfort zone. Saying no is easy. I wonder, What if God said no to us as many times as we say no to God?

Saying yes to God and being active in God's work helps us grow spiritually. This doesn't necessarily mean being seen and heard. We can all serve in quiet and humble ways known only to God. We have many opportunities to do so. Discipleship means being a servant and, as Jesus showed us, putting others ahead of ourselves.

I'm trying to respond when I hear God's call. It's hard sometimes, heeding God's voice. But when we do we receive great blessings.

Prayer: *God, help me to be a disciple who is not merely a spectator. Amen.*

Thought for the Day: When and where have I said yes to God?

Ed Williams (Alabama)

With Fresh Eyes

Read Genesis 1:28-31
The steadfast love of the LORD never ceases, his mercies never come to an end; they are new every morning; great is your faithfulness.
Lamentations 3:22-23 (NRSV)

I opened Grandma's blinds, hoping to get more light into the room. She never remembered to open them. Since moving into the dementia-care unit of this nursing home, she had become more and more forgetful. I was sad to see her slipping away.

One day we sat at her table, putting together a child's jigsaw puzzle. I had brought her flowers, and each time she looked up, she saw the flowers as if for the first time and asked me who had brought them. When I saw her look up from the puzzle yet again, I got ready to quash my irritation at the question I knew was coming.

'Well, look what someone brought!' Grandma said with pleased surprise. Then she added, 'What a beautiful day this is!'

I felt my breath catch in my throat. Grandma was remembering something I had forgotten: the beauty of what God has made. What I saw earlier as sad I now saw as amazing: a woman seeing things with fresh eyes, eyes that did not take for granted 'the ordinary'. It was as if I suddenly sensed God's abundance where I had expected only loss. Grandma gave me a glimpse of the God who dwells in those corners of life that we might call 'empty', the God who moves in darkness as well as in the light, blessing us all.

Prayer: *Show us, O God, how to live in your light, even in the dark places. Amen.*

Thought for the Day: God's Spirit carries blessing into every corner of creation.

Callie Smith (Indiana)

PRAYER FOCUS: THOSE SUFFERING FROM DEMENTIA

God's Lifeline

Read Romans 10:8-17 and 1 Corinthians 1:18-30

Moses said to the Israelites, 'I have set before you life and death… Now choose life, so that you and your children may live.'
Deuteronomy 30:19 (NIV)

A documentary on television showed a US Coast Guard helicopter rescuing two people who had been lost at sea for three torturous days and nights. Their commercial fishing boat had capsized in a violent storm that killed the rest of the crew. As the two survivors were pulled to safety, I could not only see but also feel their gratefulness and jubilation. They were saved from the threat of death.

After watching this dramatic event, I began to think of how God seeks to rescue the lost. Rescue workers cast lifelines to victims in distress. In a spiritual sense, God does the same for each of us, offering us eternal life. Can you imagine anyone who would refuse to be rescued from death?

Every day millions of people remain lost, cast adrift or separated from relationship with our loving Saviour, Christ Jesus. As believers, as those who have been rescued, we have the privilege and responsibility to offer God's lifeline to those in danger of drowning in life's turbulent seas. For them it is a matter of life or death.

Prayer: *Abba Father, remind us each day to share the good news of the life you offer to all of us. By your Spirit guide us to those who need the lifeline of your saving love. Amen.*

Thought for the Day: How and when have you thrown a lifeline by sharing your faith?

Donald L. Maly (Texas)

Joy In Living

Read 1 Samuel 16:1-13

The LORD said to Samuel, 'Do not look on his appearance or on the height of his stature, because I have rejected him; for the LORD does not see as mortals see; they look on the outward appearance, but the LORD looks on the heart.' 1 Samuel 16:7 (NRSV)

A peal of laughter rang from the hallway where my 16-year-old brother Josh was playing with his toy cat. Dad said, 'Kitty must have told a good joke.' Josh's sudden bursts of laughter no longer surprise us.

When my brother was born four-and-a-half-months prematurely, our family adapted to many things. Some adjustments tired our bodies and spirits: long hospital stays, machines beeping late in the night, the daily responsibility of caring for a dependent person whether we felt able or not. But over time we have also become accustomed to uninhibited laughter, wholehearted smiles, and living with someone who claps to every song on the radio and relishes bumpy car rides.

Many people quickly judge the abilities of others based on their appearance. The prophet Samuel saw a young, inexperienced shepherd when he first saw David. But God saw a king. When some people look at my brother, they may see someone with few abilities and little to offer. I think God sees Josh as someone with the gift of sharing the joy of living.

Prayer: *O Lord, may we see all people and their potential through your eyes. Amen.*

Thought for the Day: Look for God in the unexpected.

Ashley Barrett (Indiana)

PRAYER FOCUS: THOSE LIMITED BY THE JUDGEMENT OF OTHERS

Strong Again

Read Hebrews 3:12-14
Jesus said, 'I have told you this so that you will have peace by being united to me. The world will make you suffer. But be brave! I have defeated the world!' John 16:33 (GNB)

After 32 years of marriage, my husband wanted a divorce. I was devastated and felt that this was not God's will for our lives. I felt defeated, rejected and unloved, wondering if I was even important to God anymore.

I knew that in this troubled time, my faith was crucial. I needed and wanted to stay in touch with God through reading scripture and praying. God also used my friends and my family to encourage me and to remind me how important I am to God — so important that God sent Jesus to die for me. How much more important could I be? One of my friends would even phone me and read scripture to me because she genuinely cared for me. When I lay down at night and wiped the tears from my eyes, I felt God's arms around me. I thanked God for caring and for giving me faithful Christian friends.

Isaiah 40:31 tells us that those who trust the Lord will become strong again. God has made me strong again and has given me a desire to help others in their troubled times. Knowing that God would never betray me was and is my source of strength. No one will ever have a problem-free life. But faith in God and in our worth as beloved children of God will give us the hope and encouragement we need to remain strong and to witness to others for Christ.

Prayer: *O God, I want to put all my trust and faith in you so that I can offer encouragement to others when they face troubled times. Amen.*

Thought for the Day: I can be a blessing to someone else even in my time of trouble. *Debbie Gillis (South Carolina)*

Take A Break!

Read Matthew 6:25-34
How sweet are your words to my taste, sweeter than honey to my mouth!
Psalm 119:103 (NRSV)

The honeybee is known for its ceaseless labour. Its hive is a hotbed of activity. No wonder. A single worker bee makes 1/12th of a teaspoon of honey in her lifetime, and a good hive will produce 50 to 60 pounds of honey to survive the winter. The work never ends!

Still, it's a little known fact that even the hard-working honeybee will find a place on the comb, cease all activity — and do absolutely nothing for a while! Nothing productive as far as the world is concerned. But this time of refreshment and renewal is absolutely essential. Bees seem to require a little time away from the busyness of life, and it doesn't seem to hurt the hive at all.

Many of us discover that our levels of stress and anxiety rise because of the never-ending tasks that fill our days. We worry about whether we can keep up. During these moments I find it best to follow the example of the honeybee — and also Jesus, by the way, who went up the mountain to pray when he was very busy — and simply stop. Create a space for God to talk. And then listen.

Prayer: *Lord, we open our hearts to you. We stop to listen and learn from you. Amen.*

Thought for the Day: I cannot make a moment of time, but I can give time back to God.

Frank Ramirez (Pennsylvania)

What's in a Name?

Read Ephesians 5:1-10
A good name is to be chosen rather than great riches.
Proverbs 22:1 (NRSV)

I had gone to college and moved away from my tiny hometown of 300 people. Once when I went back to visit, I went to a neighbouring small town to shop. I was going to make a purchase and then remembered I had an out-of-state cheque.

'Will you accept a cheque from another state?' I asked the assistant. I already had my cheque book open.

She looked at my last name, Bothof, which is not an ordinary name. 'Are you John's daughter?' she asked.

'No, I'm Henry's daughter, from Chandler. John is my uncle.'

'No problem,' she said.

I wrote the cheque. Because my uncle had built a good reputation, I also was trusted. And my cheque was good; I did not shame my uncle or my father.

I have another name: Christian. I belong to the family of Christ. Christ built a reputation, and I am to follow in his steps. In my daily life, do I reflect his character? I want people to be drawn to Christ because of me.

Do my daily behaviour and my character bring shame or honour to the name Christian?

Prayer: *God, let our light shine so that when others see our good works, they will give glory to you. Amen.*

Thought for the Day: If all Christians behaved as I do, would people want to follow Christ?

Diann Bothof Lopez (Arizona)

Entwined

Read Ecclesiastes 4:9-12
Love must be sincere. Hate what is evil; cling to what is good.
Romans 12:9 (NIV)

A regular part of our vegetable gardening is to ensure that the tall pea plants are entwined through the wire mesh trellis for support. I poke the curly tendrils through the wire until they cling and grip, knowing that in time as they grow they will become firmly attached and support the whole plant. Often tendrils from the outer plants twine around stronger plants that are closer to the trellis and stabilised by the strength of the mesh.

Pea plants have hollow stems that are easily bent and broken by strong winds or by being knocked over. The trellis is absolutely essential; otherwise the plants would be constantly fractured and the nutrients could not reach the flowers. Nor would we ever harvest the pea pods!

The fragile pea plant reminds me to cling to the support we find in God's word and to learn from those with strong faith. In a world where the winds of troubles and sorrows threaten our faith, we can reach out with tendrils of prayer. God's word provides us with support and strength to withstand trials, to grow in our faith and to produce a harvest.

Prayer: *Dear God, thank you for feeding our bodies with good food and for nurturing our souls through your word. Help us to look to you for strength for each day. In Jesus' name. Amen.*

Thought for the Day: Intertwined with other believers, we are strong.

Ann Sloane (New South Wales, Australia)

The Tradition Continues

Read 2 Corinthians 12:1-10
The Lord said to Paul, 'My power is greatest when you are weak.'
2 Corinthians 12:9 (GNB)

My father-in-law, Paul, is 97 years old. When he was 79, he made a pact with God: 'If you let me live to be 80, I'll sing a solo in church.' On his 80th birthday Paul sang his first solo ever: 'How great thou art'. The congregation's response was so positive that they insisted he sing a 'birthday solo' every year.

This year, two months before his birthday, Paul suffered a stroke, weakening his right side and affecting his ability to speak clearly. While he was in the hospital, Paul managed to let his nurses know of his annual solo. Whenever they'd ask him to sing for them, he would — all three verses of the song he had been planning to sing!

When Paul came home, we wondered if he would be able to sing his solo in church this year. It would not be possible for him to work with the accompanist, and he needed a walking frame to stand. We sensed that Paul's long tradition had ended. Then God nudged me: Have Paul sing his solo for the church just as he has been singing it for the nurses at the hospital — *a cappella*. So the Sunday after his 97th birthday, Paul stood with his walking frame and sang without accompaniment and from memory: 'Precious Lord, take my hand… I am tired, I am weak, I am worn… Take my hand, precious Lord, lead me home.'

Even though Paul's body is frail, with God's power at work within him, Paul is able to continue to sing of God's presence.

Prayer: *Precious Lord, when we are tired and see no way to go on, remind us that you will always make a way for us. Amen.*

Thought for the Day: When we are weak, God is strong.

Tom Page (North Carolina)

Faith and Prayer

Read Matthew 7:7-11

Ask, and it will be given you; search, and you will find; knock, and the door will be opened for you. Matthew 7:7 (NRSV)

One autumn day my sister and I went to court to be present at the divorce proceedings of our parents. I was not taking it as hard as my sister. I was calm because in my opinion the divorce was the best solution for them. I knew we were all in God's hands; at the same time, I was a bit anxious because the court would decide the issue of custody. I didn't know where my sister and I would be living, but I knew God would be with us.

My anxiety level rose when a barrister said that he would call on my sister and me during the proceedings. After we had answered some questions, all we could do was to wait outside the courtroom. As I began to think about all the legalities, I also began to think about what God wanted for our future. At that moment I decided to pray and turn this situation and everything about it over to God. This simple prayer came to my lips: Dear God, I have faith in you and in your plans. God answered my prayer by giving me a sense of peace and confidence about the future.

Prayer: *Almighty God, in difficult times strengthen our faith. As Jesus taught us, we pray, 'Our Father which art in heaven, Hallowed be thy name. Thy kingdom come. Thy will be done in earth, as it is in heaven. Give us this day our daily bread. And forgive us our debts, as we forgive our debtors. And lead us not into temptation, but deliver us from evil: For thine is the kingdom, and the power, and the glory, for ever. Amen.'**

Thought for the Day: Faith and prayer are powerful tools in times of struggle.

Juan Carlos Carrillo (Kentucky)

PRAYER FOCUS: CHILDREN OF DIVORCED PARENTS

*Matthew 6:9-13, KJV

Hands Building Hope

Read 2 Corinthians 8:1-5
Contribute to the needs of the saints; extend hospitality to strangers.
Romans 12:13 (NRSV)

On 13 June, 2005, the northern part of Chile suffered a massive earthquake — 7.9 on the Richter scale. Many families lost their homes and all their possessions.

As we saw our people suffering, we started a campaign to help them. We brought together 30 volunteers from different cities to help to build new houses for those who had lost everything.

After a week of intense work, weariness and heat, we realised that we had not only helped to build homes but had also helped to build hope, happiness, friendship and love. It was amazing to see how our weariness could give rest to others and how our work could turn moments of darkness into beautiful daylight.

Jesus calls us to serve and help those in need. Because of him we can confront the suffering and pain that stand before us and say without question, 'Here I am, Lord' (Isa. 6:8, NRSV).

Prayer: *Lord, give us strength and courage to be obedient to your call. May our lives be used to give hope to those who have none. Amen.*

Thought for the Day: Small actions can give hope to the hopeless.

Fabiola Grandon (Santiago, Chile)

Thriving in the Pit

Read Genesis 37:23-28, 39:1-23
The LORD was with Joseph and showed him steadfast love.
Genesis 39:21 (NRSV)

Three years ago I found myself in a deep 'pit' when I was falsely accused and threatened with legal action. One certainty in life is that will find ourselves in the pit at some time. For one young mother the pit is a terminal illness. For a middle-aged man, it is the loss of a job or financial disaster. And for a fragile teenage girl, it is a broken relationship.

No one knew more about surviving in the pit than Joseph. His own brothers cast him into a well and then sold him into the slavery. Later he was falsely accused and thrown into prison. Yet Joseph not only survived but also actually thrived in his miserable circumstances.

The statement 'The LORD was with him' appears several times in today's Bible reading. The scripture seems to imply that Joseph was able to face misfortune because he knew he was not alone. Joseph understood that the Lord was with him and would deliver him (see Acts 7:9-10). How comforting it is for Christians to know that in whatever 'pit' we may find ourselves — the death of a loved one, health issues, broken relationships, or financial problems — God is with us and able to lift us out.

Prayer: *Father, as we wrestle with the struggles of life, make us keenly aware of your presence and abundant mercy. Amen.*

Thought for the Day: No pit is too deep or problem too large for God.

Terry Thomas Bowman (North Carolina)

PRAYER FOCUS: THOSE SUFFERING MISFORTUNE

Be Still

Read Psalm 46

Jesus said, 'Peace I leave with you; my peace I give you. I do not give to you as the world gives. Do not let your hearts be troubled and do not be afraid.' John 14:27 (NIV)

Life seems increasingly busy. In a major railway station during rush hour, hundreds of people are in transit, rushing to reach their destinations. On board trains or buses, everyone is talking on mobile telephones. At the shopping centre or supermarket, people buy as if the shops were going to close at any moment. When we call a friend on the telephone, we often get the answering machine. Should our lives be like this: constant rushing, never a quiet moment, always listening to or watching some electronic device?

Jesus knew that it was vital to withdraw from the crowds to gain strength for his task and peace for his soul. He knew that time spent with God, listening as well as talking, was needed to continue the work he came to do. We're no different. We need moments of peace in our busy days and time to spend with God, to rest in God's arms, to be still in God's presence. That quiet makes a difference in our life.

Prayer: *God, help us to follow Jesus' example, finding peace and stillness in our busy lives. May we never be too busy or too preoccupied to listen to your voice. Amen.*

Thought for the Day: In times of quiet, we can listen for the voice of God.

Ann Lockwood (Sheffield, England)

Unburdened?

Read Luke 18:18-29

[Jesus] said to [the ruler], 'You still lack one thing. Sell everything you have… Then come, follow me.' Luke 18:22 (NIV)

The words of Jesus in Luke 18 are often misunderstood as an indictment of the rich and a call for us to sell all our possessions. To read it only in this way is to miss an important message. Jesus sees that the man wants more out of life than possessions can bring him, so he offers him a solution that will bring him peace and fulfilment. Jesus simply tells him to cast aside his burdens and follow him. The man rejected the change Jesus called for either because he did not believe that the solution would work or because he saw changing as more painful than staying as he was. The man came to Jesus wanting a closer relationship with God, but he lacked the belief and trust that Jesus could fulfil all his needs and desires.

Whether we are rich or poor, believing that God can and will meet our needs and show us the way is the key to living a life of meaning and purpose. Jesus models deep and abiding trust in God, and his teachings show us the way to life. However, it is up to us and our free will to accept or reject the offer. Jesus does not beg the man to follow or explain why he should. Instead, he uses the situation to point out that those who are not burdened by possessions find it easier to gain trust and peace as they follow Christ.

Prayer: *Lord, may we place our burdens on you and trust that every-thing we seek can be found in serving you. Amen.*

Thought for the Day: Do I spend more time taking care of my pos-sessions than I spend with God?

Mark H. Anderson (Pennsylvania)

PRAYER FOCUS: THOSE WORRIED ABOUT DEBT AND POSSESSIONS

Just For Me

Read Exodus 16:11-18

My God shall supply all your need according to his riches in glory by Christ Jesus. Philippians 4:19 (KJV)

When I met my friend Jan many years ago, she was one of the nicest people I had met, but she didn't know Jesus Christ. One of the blessings in my life has been watching the transformation that has taken place since Jan came to know Christ as her personal Saviour. One of the tools she has used to help her grow as a Christian is *The Upper Room*. Our standing joke is to say that each daily meditation was written with us in mind: 'I don't know what your *Upper Room* said today, but mine definitely was written just for me.' Recently, on my birthday, I had the last laugh because the Prayer Focus was for 'those celebrating a birthday today'.

Although Jan and I joke about it, the truth is that God does know what each of us needs for each day. God can and does speak to each of our hearts through the words we read, the smile of a stranger, a phone call from a friend, and many other encounters that help us with individual needs and problems. We need only be open to the Holy Spirit and aware of the 'coincidences' that take place in our daily lives to hear God speak to us or see God's hand at work.

Prayer: *Thank you, God, for providing what we need. Help us to be so in tune with the Holy Spirit that we never overlook your gifts of love and guidance. Amen.*

Thought for the Day: What is God's word to you in today's devotional time?

Donna Heizer (Kentucky)

To Conquer

Read Revelation 3:11-13

In all these things we are more than conquerors through him who loved us. Romans 8:37 (NRSV)

As a child, I tried to imitate my weekly comic-magazine heroes; I was ready to wage battle armed with a wooden sword, a cork shield and a vivid imagination. After I heard a bit about the book of Revelation, my curiosity drove me to read it. I got as far as the third chapter. The fantasy aspects of the book grew and grew in my mind as I realised that the conqueror always received the prize.

I asked an adult, 'Who is the enemy I need to vanquish?'

'Sin,' was the response.

How dangerous it must be, I thought, to confront this foe! I will have to use my sword, my shield and, if necessary, my fists.

Today, I continue to think about the word conquer. Over time, I have become convinced that the most subtle enemy is the one that, in a thousand ways, attempts to turn us away from being constant in prayer; from reading and meditating on the Bible; from attending church; and from rejoicing, praising and adoring God. Let us be ever alert to invisible but powerful pressure to change our focus. And let us continually turn our gaze back to Christ, the author and finisher of our faith (see Heb. 12:2).

Prayer: *Lord, strengthen our decision to live as faithful disciples. Amen.*

Thought for the Day: Christ calls us to stand firm and to be faithful.

Sergio Gomez (Alicante, Spain)

PRAYER FOCUS: BELIEVERS FACING GREAT TEMPTATION

Our Father

Read Psalm 19:1-6

[Jesus] said unto [his disciples], 'When ye pray, say, Our Father…'
Luke 11:2 (KJV)

As a child of about five, I looked up in awe at the bright stars flickering against winter's dark sky. My warm breath made momentary shallow clouds above me as I shivered in January's chill. Mum and my two older sisters were just steps ahead of my dad and me as we crossed the country road in front of our vicarage, on the way to a bring-and-share supper at church. My dad held my hand snug in one hand while balancing a dish of steaming potatoes in the other.

Darkness always frightened me except when my dad was near. Even in those earliest scenes in my life, I felt safe and peaceful when he was nearby. He had a strong trust in God's faithfulness and love, and he lived confidently in that assurance. Dad helped me grow in the shelter of God's love and set my feet on a path that led me to find my own way to my heavenly Father.

When Jesus invites us to call God Father, wonderful images of my dad remind me of the tender love God has for us. God welcomes us to take his hand and walk on in the shelter of his presence. Even the greatest example of a dad's love for his child can't compare to the depth of love God has for each of us.

Prayer: *Dear God, show us what it means to know you as a loving Father, that we may live as your dearly loved children. In Jesus' name. Amen.*

Thought for the Day: I am and will always be a child of God.

Dori Magee (New York)

The Christian Mystery

Read 1 Corinthians 2:1-5

We have been buried with him by baptism into death, so that, just as Christ was raised from the dead by the glory of the Father, so we too might walk in newness of life. Romans 6:4 (NRSV)

I was almost 18 years old that Sunday morning as I gathered with over one hundred young people to pray. I was there because I had died the night before, not from a physical crisis but from a spiritual crisis. Even though I accepted Christ as my Saviour at the age of 11, later I had decided to live by the values of my high-school friends rather than my Christian friends.

This particular weekend, I was attending a Christian youth seminar. On Saturday night a young former-motorcycle-gang member shared his testimony of how God had changed his life. He convinced me that half-hearted Christianity was no longer an option. Jesus was either the Lord of all — or he was not Lord at all. Jesus' death and resurrection were the pattern and the price of discipleship. I decided to follow Christ — with my whole heart and life.

The sense of forgiveness and reconciliation this gave me came only after a slow death as I crucified my pride and dependence on peer approval. My resurrection was slow as well, like the rising of the sun — gradual and illuminating. That was 40 years ago, and my life in Christ has not been easy. But is has been fresh and 'new every morning' (Lam. 3:23).

Prayer: *Lord Jesus, thank you for showing me the way through death to life in the power of your Spirit. Amen.*

Thought for the Day: Christian faith demands our whole heart and life.

Thomas R. Albin (Tennessee)

Cries for Help

Read Psalm 86:1-8

In the day of my trouble I call on you, for you will answer me.
Psalm 86:7 (NRSV)

My sister has schizophrenia, a chronic mental condition with symptoms of both mood disorder and psychosis. Despite regular medication and visits to the psychiatrist over the past 30 years, she still experiences periods of extreme mood swings. We as family members have to take care of her, and that has brought us much suffering in her times of trouble.

Over the years, I have come to experience a total trust in the Lord. When my sister seems out of control, I kneel beside my bed and earnestly pray for help. I pray for the Lord to let the Holy Spirit fill her. Realising that during these moments of agony there is no medication to help her any further, I also pray for the Lord's healing power and guidance, to give me wisdom to communicate with her at the right time. Often after a moment my sister calms down, and the outcome of these episodes is usually better than I expect.

As children of God, we are blessed to know that God does hear our prayers. Sometimes we may panic when there is a crisis. However, if we call out in prayer, we will find that God is always there to help us and give us peace.

Prayer: *Dear God, thank you for answering our prayers in times of trouble when we have exhausted our human abilities. May we learn to trust you totally in every moment of our life. Amen.*

Thought for the Day: God hears and answers our cries for help.

Doris Yeung (Samut Prakan, Thailand)

Room at the Table

Read Luke 22:14-23

When the hour came, [Jesus] took his place at the table, and the apostles with him. Luke 22:14 (NRSV)

When our sons were young, we received a dinner invitation from friends. Assuming that the invitation included the boys, we took them with us. When we arrived, the host and hostess warmly welcomed us into their home. As we settled in, I noticed only four settings at the dinner table.

After a time of warm fellowship, our hostess invited all of us to the table. I noticed that she had added two settings. Quietly she had made room for our sons. Although she had not included them in her invitation, as we had assumed, she wanted them to be included at the table. She never mentioned to us the error in our assumption.

Over the years since then, I have thought about how Jesus made room at the table for all of his disciples. He did not exclude from the table Judas, who would later betray him, or Peter, who would soon deny him three times. Instead, Jesus included all of the disciples in his Passover meal, knowing full well that later they would desert him in order to save their own lives. This helps me to see that if God made a place for all of them, then there is also a place at God's table for you and me.

Prayer: *God of grace and glory, thank you for inviting and welcoming all of us to your table. Amen.*

Thought for the Day: God's table is big enough for every one of us.

Ernest S. Lyght (West Virginia)

Turning Over Our Doubts

Read Mark 9:14-27

Trust in the Lord with all your heart and lean not on your own understanding; in all your ways acknowledge him, and he will make your paths straight. Proverbs 3:5-6 (NIV)

After years of striving to walk with Christ, I arrived at a place in my spiritual journey where doubts and insecurities had become obstacles in my path. I found myself wondering if what I had believed all my life was in fact true. My mind and heart were full of questions like, 'Is the Bible really the word of God?' and 'Does God really love me unconditionally?' I was desperate to believe again, but like the father in Mark 9:24 I had to accept that I needed the Lord's help with my unbelief. All my striving would not remove these roadblocks to my faith.

With a graduate degree in the sciences, I had always relied on my ability to reason. However, feeling overwhelmed by doubt and confusion taught me a humbling lesson: There are some things that I just cannot work out. Isn't that what faith is all about — believing in something beyond our limited powers of observation and reason?

Like the father described in Mark 9, I had to become desperate enough to cry out, 'Help my unbelief' (Mark 9:24, NRSV) — and in mercy, Christ has answered my cry.

Prayer: *Lord Jesus Christ, thank you for your unconditional love for us, even when we struggle with unbelief. Help us to give our doubts to you, mindful of your grace and mercy. Amen.*

Thought for the Day: Grace is not a puzzle to be solved but a gift to be embraced.

Diane Chambers (New Jersey)

Awaiting the Sunrise

Read Acts 2:42-47

It is good for me to draw near to God: I have put my trust in the LORD GOD, that I may declare all thy works. Psalm 73:28 (KJV)

This has been an extraordinary season for hummingbirds in our area. During my devotional time each morning, the hummingbirds arrive at the feeder full of sweetened water that I have placed outside my window. I enjoy watching one of my favourites of God's creatures as I await the sunrise.

One day I noticed that the hummingbirds did not arrive. The feeder was empty. In my busy-ness, I had forgotten to refill it. I was concerned that the hummingbirds had gone elsewhere. I quickly refilled their feeder, and within minutes it was again abuzz with hummingbirds enjoying the food and life as they drank and chased each other around my garden.

So it is with us as we are nourished by studying the Bible. When we live in the life-giving nourishment of God's word, we enjoy the satisfaction that only spiritual intimacy can bring. When this intimacy is absent from our lives because we have neglected our relationship with God, life seems empty and we long to experience again God's presence. When we return and take in spiritual food, we can join others who seek relationship with our Creator.

Prayer: *Father God, thank you for providing the spiritual nourishment we desperately need and for placing within us the desire for it. In Jesus' name we pray. Amen.*

Thought for the Day: Maintaining spiritual intimacy with God feeds us and allows us to feed others.

J. Reid Mowrer (New Mexico)

PRAYER FOCUS: THOSE LONGING FOR DEEPER INTIMACY WITH GOD

Special Care

Read John 15:1-11

Jesus said, 'I am the vine, you are the branches. Those who abide in me and I in them bear much fruit, because apart from me you can do nothing.' John 15:5 (NRSV)

Two rose bushes in my garden are a true gift from God. They are planted close to the house, and I have a perfect view of them. I can see and enjoy these plants all the time, especially when they are in bloom.

A few days ago, in a bit of a rush, I cut a few flowers and placed them temporarily in a container with water. Several hours later, I decided to transfer them to a vase. Much to my dismay, two short-stemmed blooms were drooping and lifeless. I quickly noticed that the stems of these two plants did not reach the water level. Consequently, these roses did not look fresh as the other ones with longer stems did.

I began to think about Jesus' words in John 15:5: 'Apart from me you can do nothing.' There are those among us who are fragile. They too are God's children. We have a responsibility to care for them by offering the Living Water, Jesus Christ, through our love, witness, prayer and wise counsel. When we help them to find this Water, these fragile ones can grow stronger and bear beautiful flowers, as they were meant to.

Prayer: *Lord, help us to extend special care to those who are starting the Christian journey. Amen.*

Thought for the Day: Spend time helping others to find the Living Water.

Blanca B. de Melimán (Buenos Aires, Argentina)

Problems on Parade

Read Psalm 63

All [mortals'] days are full of pain, and their work is a vexation; even at night their minds do not rest. Ecclesiastes 2:23 (NRSV)

When I awake in the night, my mind sometimes tends to race. That's when my 'problems on parade' prevent me from going back to sleep. Events of the day revisit me, disrupting my slumber and turning me into a tossing, turning, sheet-pulling worrier.

It's 2 a.m. and the battle that has been raging in my mind has now switched to a struggle for sleep. After some time, my pleadings for the rest I deserve and need become demands.

But, finally surrendering, I begin to pray. I've learned to be specific and direct in praying for each situation that has been nagging at me. One by one, each 'float' in the parade of problems is removed from the line with the words: 'Thy will be done, not mine.' Instead of clinging to my wisdom and my human solutions, I visualise myself placing each problem in God's hands. I actively, deliberately 'leave all [my] worries with [God] because he cares for [me]' (1 Pet. 5:7, GNB). And sometimes even before I finish the list, I am asleep again.

In the morning some of the same problems may come back to mind. When that happens, I remind myself often and prayerfully that I have turned them over to God.

Prayer: *Lord, it is hard to let go of problems, even knowing who you are and how much you care. Forgive us for trying to do work of which only you are capable. We place in your care our need for rest. Amen.*

Thought for the Day: When problems parade, remember that God is near — and pray.

Timothy J. Nadeau (New Mexico)

PRAYER FOCUS: PEOPLE WITH SLEEP DISORDERS

Roadside Grace

Read Matthew 25:31-40

The king will answer [the righteous], 'Truly I tell you, just as you did it to one of the least of these who are members of my family, you did it to me.'
Matthew 25:40 (NRSV)

The man stood on a street corner at the edge of the city. He sold newspapers to drivers stopped at the traffic-lights, hobbling from car to car, a crutch under one arm and newspapers under the other. He had only one leg and walked with a rusty crutch. His front teeth did not match.

At first I shrank in my seat as the man approached each driver to try to sell a paper. Ashamed of my fear, I decided to pray for him instead of cringe. And I began to buy a paper from him every Thursday on my way to visit my elderly uncle.

After a few months, I missed three straight Thursdays. Overdue projects at work, a family crisis, and hacking bronchitis kept me from my visits to my uncle. Finally back to my regular schedule, I reached his corner, where the light stopped me as usual. I gave the newspaper seller my dollar and told him of my recent woes. His face softened. He stuffed his papers under one arm and laid his hand on my arm. Then he said, 'I pray you'll be better soon.' I took in a big breath. I, who have enough teeth to eat a good meal and two whole legs to take me anywhere, received the gift of comfort in his prayer, simply offered before the traffic-light changed. Christ had a new face, and I rejoiced to see him on the roadside.

Prayer: *Dear God, open our eyes to your presence in places we least expect. Amen.*

Thought for the Day: Today I will look for Christ in each one I meet.
Linda Tatum (North Carolina)

My Father

Read Psalm 27:1-10

If my father and mother forsake me, the LORD will take me up.
Psalm 27:10 (NRSV)

My parents separated when I was three years old, making it very difficult for my mother to bring up my brother and me. My father supported us financially, but his love was missing.

Many years later we were able to demonstrate our love for him when he was in prison. We visited him and looked after our other brothers and sisters, his children from a second marriage.

Fortunately, I came to know God and to accept God as my Father. I knew I was God's child, blessed by having bestowed on me all the paternal love that had been lacking in my childhood. The gift of God's love enabled me to love my earthly father more and to let go of resentment.

I have discovered that God is and always will be my refuge. When my earthly parents are no longer with me, I know I can count on God, whose love is eternal.

Prayer: *Father, teach us to love you as you love us. We pray as Jesus taught us, saying, 'Our Father which art in heaven, Hallowed be thy name. Thy kingdom come. Thy will be done in earth, as it is in heaven. Give us this day our daily bread. And forgive us our debts, as we forgive our debtors. And lead us not into temptation, but deliver us from evil: For thine is the kingdom, and the power, and the glory, for ever. Amen.'*

Thought for the Day: God's love is constant and forever.

Yohanis Zapata Rodríguez (Holguín, Cuba)

PRAYER FOCUS: CHILDREN OF THOSE IN PRISON

*Matthew 6:9-13, KJV

A Wonderful Gift

Read Job 19:23-27

Moses said unto the people, Remember this day, in which ye came out from Egypt, out of the house of bondage; for by strength of hand the LORD brought you out from this place. Exodus 13:3 (KJV)

A few years ago, I began to keep a journal. I had tried for several years before, but when I finally committed myself, I realised that keeping a journal is not a task for completion but a wonderful opportunity for self-expression, reflection and release.

Job knew the value of writing. He expresses sorrow and laments that his words have not been written down: 'Oh that my words were now written! oh that they were printed in a book!' (Job 19:23-24, KJV).

Keeping a journal has been a life-changing experience for me. I take time to record important events in my life and even the mundane occurrences of my day. I am able to express my deepest feelings and concerns and to link my life to verses of scripture about God's grace and mercy, which offer deliverance.

As I read over my journals, I recall with great fondness many of the joys of my life. When my writing reflects the sorrows and pain I have experienced, my journal also serves as a reminder of the mighty works of our Lord and Saviour, and God's divine love for me. Remembering God's grace and acts of deliverance strengthens my faith.

Writing is a wonderful gift that we give ourselves.

Prayer: *Gracious God, thank you for grace that brings us through the joys as well as the trials of life. Continue to strengthen our faith each day. Amen.*

Thought for the Day: Take time today to remember how God has acted in your life.

Marcia Conston (North Carolina)

God-forsaken?

Read 1 John 4:16-21

The king will answer, 'I was sick and you took care of me.'
Matthew 25:36 (NRSV)

Before I went to Somalia as a journalist, I was told it is a God-forsaken country. It's hot, dry and lacks amenities such as electricity and running water. I visited a small hospital, really only open-air cinder-block rooms, that lacked even rudimentary supplies. There I met two Muslim physicians, both volunteers.

One of their patients was a severely injured aid worker who had driven onto one of the land mines that litter much of the region. Across the hall was a terribly burned young woman whose hut caught fire after a bomb she had been hiding for a rebel group exploded. The physician tending her spoke softly, swabbing the young woman's wounds with great tenderness.

As in so many places, death and destruction rain down far too easily there. But in the midst of terror and pain, between a peacemaker and a guerrilla, I watched this doctor risking his life to bring wholeness. I heard compassion in his voice and saw it in his healing touch. I felt that I stood in the presence of God, and I knew that God has not forsaken this place — or any place of suffering and pain.

Prayer: *O God, we never know where we will find you or in whose face you will appear. Keep us mindful that you are present even in places we've been told you have forsaken. Help us to see your steadfast love in every face and every place. Amen.*

Thought for the Day: God is with each one who suffers and with each one who offers help.

Larry Hollon (Tennessee)

New Horizons

Read Jeremiah 29:11-13

Jesus said, 'I came that they may have life, and have it abundantly.'
John 10:10 (NRSV)

Children have fun blowing the seeds off a dandelion and watching them float away in all directions. Sometimes the children are disappointed when the fun is over; they want the heads back in one piece so they can experience it all again. But no amount of glue could put a dandelion together again in the way it was created. This dispersal of the dandelion head occurs for a reason: it maximises the chances of one of the seeds finding a suitable place to set down roots and continue the life cycle. The simple act of letting go and allowing the forces of life to propel it is an integral part of life for dandelions.

When life blows us in new directions or propels us into a new stage, we often become uneasy. We may try to cling to the familiar rather than holding on tightly to life and allowing change to carry us along new paths. Fear of the unknown overwhelms many of us, preventing us from enjoying life in all its abundance. However, God calls us towards new horizons, new adventures and new paths.

We may feel at times as if we are being blown apart, just like the dandelion head. God, however, already has a place prepared where we can put down roots and bloom afresh.

Prayer: *Lord, as our paths change, help us to seek your guidance. Help us to put our trust in you, wherever we may be. Amen.*

Thought for the Day: Life's winds blow us to new places and towards new growth.

Meg Mangan (New South Wales, Australia)

Coming Home

Read Luke 15:11-24

While [the prodigal] was still far off, his father saw him and... ran and put his arms around him. Luke 15: 20 (NRSV)

A week from today my family will fly north and then drive two hours to a reunion with four generations of the Harnish family. We'll drive past the farm where my dad's parents raised seven children. We'll visit the hillside cemetery where my mother's parents are buried. We'll worship in the church where I was baptised. My daughters will patiently endure and laugh at the stories we all tell — again. Still, that place is no longer my home.

I know that for far too many, home is a place of fear, rejection, abuse and pain that haunts them. But the idea of home goes deeper than our memories and experiences. Home is not so much a place as it is a longing. At its depths, the longing for home brings us to recognise our deep, spiritual homesickness for God.

One of Jesus' most familiar and loved parables is the story of two sons, one who went away and one who stayed at home. Most of all, it's the story of our loving God who longs for each of us to come home. Our deep spiritual hungers are satisfied only by relationship with God, and we are all homeless without it. But like the father in Jesus' story, God watches for us and comes running to welcome us into that relationship the moment we turn towards it.

Prayer: *Welcoming Father, help us to find the home you offer us in loving relationship with you and others. Amen.*

Thought for the Day: In God we find loving and lasting welcome.

James A. Harnish (Florida)

PRAYER FOCUS: THOSE FOR WHOM HOME IS FULL OF FEAR

Summoned to the King's Table

Read 2 Samuel 9:1-13
He brought me to the banqueting house, and his intention toward me was love. Song of Solomon 2:4 (NRSV)

When I was given my first major assignment as a sportswriter, I was nervous and insecure. I didn't know how the system worked. I wasn't even sure if there would be a seat waiting for me in the press box. To make matters worse, I couldn't even find the entrance. Luckily, a kind security guard took me under her wing and showed me the ropes. She guided me into the press box and over to a row of leather seats. There in the sold-out stadium was a seat with my name on it. I relaxed and watched the game from the best seat in the house.

Mephibosheth must have felt the same kind of insecurity when he was summoned to King David's table. One day this poor, crippled man was clinging to society's bottom rung, and the next he was dining in the king's banquet hall. Though Mephibosheth probably felt fearful, it gave David pleasure to bless the son of his dear friend Jonathan. So for the rest of his life, this once-neglected man feasted to his heart's content.

We too have been invited to feast at the King's table. God invites each of us to live free of guilt and full of grace and mercy. We may feel undeserving of this honour, yet we must remember that it gives God pleasure to have us dwell with our creator. So sit back, relax and simply say yes to God's invitation.

Prayer: *Dear God, help us receive your blessings with joy and thankfulness rather than guilt and insecurity. Amen.*

Thought for the Day: It gives God great pleasure to bless us.

Alexander Marestaing (California)

Sorrow into Joy

Read Romans 8:28-39
Neither death nor life… will be able to separate us from the love of God.
Romans 8:38, 39 (NIV)

Twelve years ago, my father ended his life. He didn't say goodbye, and he didn't tell us why. His act shattered our family; for a time we wandered in confusion and doubt. It was difficult to accept that a loving God would allow something so painful to enter our lives.

We searched the Bible for hope, peace and understanding. Each day God spoke to us through scripture and through the kindness of our Christian brothers and sisters. In countless ways God provided for our daily needs when we were too devastated to care.

In Romans 8:28, Paul wrote, 'We know that in all things God works for the good of those who love him, who have been called according to his purpose' (NIV). We may never know why my father took his life. We may not in this lifetime understand why God allowed it to happen. But we are very certain of God's ability to make all things — even tragedy — work for our good.

God took the sorrow of death and turned it into a lesson about the joy of life. Today, the members of my family are careful to listen to each other more intently, to consider each other more deeply and to treasure the time we have together.

Prayer: *God of hope and peace, thank you for promising to bring good from our sorrow. In the name of the one who redeemed us all, Jesus Christ. Amen.*

Thought for the Day: Treasure each moment you have with those you love.

Maggie Silbernagel (Alabama)

PRAYER FOCUS: FAMILIES COPING WITH SUICIDE

The Greatest Gift

Read Proverbs 22:6 and Ephesians 6:1-4

Jesus said, 'Let the little children come to me, and do not hinder them, for the kingdom of heaven belongs to such as these.' Matthew 19:14 (NIV)

People often ask me at what point in my life I accepted Jesus Christ as my Saviour. I am sure my answer is often disappointing because I had no earthshaking or near-death experience that brought me to my faith. Because my parents were Christian, strong in their beliefs, I have known about Jesus and felt close to him as far back as I can recall. I remember sitting in Sunday School, looking up at pictures of Jesus holding a little child and wishing with all my heart that I could be that child sitting on Jesus' knee.

I suppose you could say that my faith was given to me by my parents the day I was born and has evolved over the years. Their gift is definitely a 'gift that keeps on giving'. Through my study of God's word, I have made my faith the foundation for the many decisions I have had to make in my life. Faith is my rock — immovable, unshakeable, unchangeable — that one thing I have been able to depend on and trust completely during the inevitable dark and tough times in life. This gift has been a priceless and precious legacy that I have joyfully handed down to our children, who are now handing it down to our grandchildren.

Although I am now in my later years, I know I am still a child of God, one of the little children Jesus still calls to and holds close.

Prayer: *Thank you, Lord, for loving Christians who teach us about you and show us how to live for and serve you. In Jesus' name we pray. Amen.*

Thought for the Day: Whom can I 'parent' in the faith today?

Anne Sheffield (Virginia)

An Incredible Peace

Read Philippians 4:1-9

The peace of God, which transcends all understanding, will guard your hearts and your minds in Christ Jesus. Philippians 4:7 (NIV)

Being transported on a trolley gave me a different perspective of the hospital where I had worked for five years. Now I was a patient. After suffering chest pains, I had taken myself to the emergency room. The cardiologist decided I needed an angiogram.

Because I was always the respiratory therapist who attended patients on life-support, I knew the procedure when my trolley was pushed into the room. The nurse was surprised to see me, but she said that she didn't have to explain the procedure since I already understood what was going to happen. She was right, but nevertheless, I began to worry.

At that moment, an incredible peace entered my heart. It was as if God said to me, 'It doesn't matter if you live or die; you are in my hands.' I discovered that peace doesn't mean the end to conflict; it simply demonstrates the love of God. And we don't have to wait for a major crisis in our lives; we can allow the peace of Christ to rule our hearts each day (see Col. 3:15).

Prayer: *Heavenly Father, we desire your peace and your love in our hearts. May we be open before you as you fill us with your love. Amen.*

Thought for the Day: Be prepared to experience God's peace.

Richard Parker (Alabama)

PRAYER FOCUS: HOSPITAL EMERGENCY STAFF

Taste and See

Read Psalm 34:1-14

O taste and see that the LORD is good; happy are those who take refuge in him. Psalm 34:8 (NRSV)

Last night I made a chicken casserole with green chillies, that had won rave reviews from my friends. My son ventured into the kitchen, asked what we were having for dinner, and turned up his nose at the unfamiliar dish.

'Taste it, and see if you like it,' I said. 'Don't base your opinion on what it looks like, what you think about the ingredients, what jokes your brother makes about it or anything else. Try it for yourself.'

Later, while I was meditating on Psalm 34:8, I thought of the casserole and my son's reaction to it. In much the same way, some people turn up their noses at religion, basing their opinion on what they hear or on what they think about someone who is religious.

We do not have to rely on what other people say about God, and we do not learn about God only by reading scripture, singing hymns or listening to sermons. Each of these is valuable, but God calls us to take another step, a step from knowledge to relationship. We build a relationship with God through spending personal time with God and by praying. As we talk to God about our lives and get to know God personally, we will see for ourselves 'that the LORD is good'.

Prayer: *Lord God, help us to move closer to you. Let us taste and see that you are good. Amen.*

Thought for the Day: Knowing about God is only the beginning of relationship with God.

Cathy Wesolek (Indiana)

The Mystery of Suffering

Read 1 Corinthians 13:8-13
Jesus said, 'Remember, I am with you always, to the end of the age.'
Matthew 28:20 (NRSV)

For centuries, theologians and philosophers have grappled with the problem of human suffering. Some regard suffering as a consequence of our sin — an explanation that cannot be dismissed entirely, for the Bible tells us, 'Do not be deceived; God is not mocked, for you reap whatever you sow' (Gal. 6:7, NRSV). Others believe that suffering can come as a test of faith, and the Bible suggests that this could on occasion be true, as in the case of Job. And the Bible tells us that at times suffering may be a learning experience, with God as our benevolent teacher (Heb. 5:8 and 12:7-11).

I have had to conclude, however, that often we cannot find an acceptable reason for suffering. Too frequently, suffering just doesn't make sense and accomplishes no good that we can see: A baby is born seriously deformed. A mother dies of breast cancer. An aeroplane crashes, killing scores of passengers.

Yet through it all, we have the promise that in our times of suffering — whatever our tribulations, however heavy our burdens, no matter what our anguish — nothing can separate us from the love of God that is in Christ Jesus our Lord (Rom. 8:35-39). With this assurance, we can find consolation and courage to move forward in faith, knowing that this world is not our home and trusting that someday the mysteries of life will be explained.

Prayer: *In our times of disappointment and despair, O God, may we feel your presence and find strength in your word. Amen.*

Thought for the Day: When troubles mount up, we can lean on God's strong arms.   *Ralph Lord Roy (Connecticut)*

PRAYER FOCUS: SOMEONE FACING TROUBLED QUESTIONS

God's Love Made Real

Read Galatians 6:1-10

Bear one another's burdens, and in this way you will fulfil the law of Christ. Galatians 6:2 (NRSV)

In our church, at the end of each school year we offer an opportunity for the young people who are leaving school and 'graduating' from the youth group to say farewell. Listening to them recently as they spoke one by one, I was both saddened and encouraged.

I was saddened because life is hard for many of them. Some have divorced parents. Others, although materially blessed, suffer deep emotional pain. All are challenged by living in a society where crime, violence and substance abuse are rife and pressure to conform is strong.

I was encouraged because I heard how the youth group provided acceptance, support and a safe, welcoming place for these young people to meet. Several confessed that without the group they might have acted out their inner loneliness in destructive behaviour. But the genuine care and love of other young people demonstrated in a tangible way the love of God.

God's love expressed through us to another can prevent tragedy, provide fulfilment, and make the difference between despair and hope.

Prayer: *God of love, help young people in the enormous challenges they face today. May they find in your people strong expressions of your love, and may this be true for all of us, young or old. Amen.*

Thought for the Day: By showing God's love, we may help someone move from despair to hope.

Sally Argent (Western Cape, South Africa)

Faith and Works

Read Philippians 3:7-14

Train yourself in godliness, for, while physical training is of some value, godliness is valuable in every way, holding promise for both the present life and the life to come. 1 Timothy 4:7-8 (NRSV)

At one time I was a tennis instructor. During this time, I learned that what I taught my students was one thing and how they applied that teaching on the court was another. Students may have understood the premise of the game and my expectations, but they struggled to put them into practice.

Is this not true with our faith as well? The Bible tells us how God wants us to live, but as we attempt to fulfil the will of God, we face challenges and ordeals.

Like the tennis novice who works to become a formidable player, we grow stronger in our faith by practising it every day. And like good students who practise their backhand and forehand, we show our faith as we obey God in real life. This is not easy. But God uses the challenges that come where we are most vulnerable in order to turn our weaknesses into strengths.

And, like a good tennis player who eventually wins a tournament, at some point we will obtain spiritual victory. When we gain the prize of victory in Christ, our hearts overflow with joy and blessing.

Prayer: *Loving God, grant us the strength to persevere in serving you. Amen.*

Thought for the Day: Keep practising your faith until you get it right.

Oscar Quiñones (Puerto Rico)

PRAYER FOCUS: THOSE FALTERING IN PRACTISING THEIR FAITH

God Knows Me

Read Psalm 139:1-18

LORD, you have examined me and you know me. You know everything I do; from far away you understand all my thoughts. Psalm 139:1-2 (GNB)

When the children are all together for our church's holiday club, the babble is deafening. They are excited, telling stories with their friends, singing and clapping from sheer exuberance. I cannot pick one voice out of the crowd.

Think about all the prayers lifted to God in a single moment. To our ears, what a babble — so many people, so many cares, so many words to tell the Lord! But God hears each specific prayer, whether it is spoken, silent, eloquent, halting, desperate or ecstatic. God hears each prayer separately, knows each person's need, and answers.

This reminds me of what I saw with the cattle on our farm. Each spring, my dad inoculated the calves, first separating them from their mothers. The din was deafening. The cows milled around outside the enclosure and the calves mingled inside it. How could they ever be sorted out and matched? But when the gates were opened, after a little jostling and a lot of bellowing, each cow and her calf moved off together at peace. In all that confusion, they were able to recognise each other through scent and sound.

God picks each of us out of the crowd. God knows every hair on our head, our voice, our scent. God rejoices over us and longs to be with us.

Prayer: *Dear God, we are amazed by your love. Help us to show your love to everyone we meet. Amen.*

Thought for the Day: God knows me and walks with me.

Donna Geiger (Virginia)

Looking for Perfection?

Read Romans 3:20-26
Surely there is no one on earth so righteous as to do good without ever sinning. Ecclesiastes 7:20 (NRSV)

I once worked as a decorator. One day while working alone inside a motel room, I stood back to admire the way I had painted a windowsill. It looked perfect. But as I leaned closer, I discovered tiny streaks where the paint was not evenly distributed. Determined to get the job not only right but perfect, I repainted the windowsill — six times. Each time, I found the tiny streaks. After 20 minutes I gave up and moved to the rest of the windowframe. At the end of the week my boss paid me without criticising the quality of my work.

Days later I thought about the windowsill and realised how unrealistic I had been. I then formulated what I call the Painter's Philosophy of Life: If you look for imperfection, you will easily find it.

Perfection is a noble goal but one which is ultimately unattainable. It's silly to expect perfection in ourselves, and it is damaging to demand perfection from the people we love — our children, our spouses, our friends. It's better to look for the honest effort, not the perfect job. Jesus knew his followers would make mistakes and even turn against him, yet he never stopped loving them. Like him, we can learn to love imperfect people.

Prayer: *Heavenly Father, thank you for forgiving us when we make mistakes and for loving us in spite of them. Amen.*

Thought for the Day: Seek perfection, but don't be consumed by the search.

Ralph Ellis (Georgia)

PRAYER FOCUS: FOR PATIENCE WITH MY IMPERFECTION

As Your Days…

Read Deuteronomy 33:24-28
As your days, so is your strength. Deuteronomy 33:25 (NRSV)

One day in May, 1979, my wife and I were travelling by car to the university where we taught when we were involved in an accident that nearly ended my life. When I next opened my eyes, I found myself in a hospital. I had been unconscious for 24 hours. During that time a doctor had begun to treat the fractures I had sustained. The most serious damage was a right hip fracture that left me unable to walk.

Upon learning this, I remembered a portion of scripture: 'As your days, so is your strength.' I could not recall where in the Bible it could be found or the full context of the passage, but this verse came to me over and over again, like a personal promise from God. With this assurance, I endured seven months of treatment, wearing a plaster-cast and confined to a wheelchair. Finally I was able to walk with a cane until I regained full use of my limbs.

After 30 years, this experience continues to fill me with awe and inspires me to trust that I will receive new strength every day from God. With this confidence, I can face hardships as I follow God's will for me in every area of my life.

Prayer: *Loving Creator, help us to remember every day that you are the source of our strength. Amen.*

Thought for the Day: God offers us strength for each new day.

Raúl Rocha (Buenos Aires, Argentina)

Undivided Worship

Read Psalm 86:8-17

Teach me your way, O LORD, and I will walk in your truth; give me an undivided heart, that I may fear your name. Psalm 86:11 (NIV)

My parents live in Hong Kong. During my first visit, my mother told me about various cultural practices I needed to know. 'When you hand someone something,' she said, 'always hold it with both hands. Using only one hand is considered rude.'

I thought it would be easy enough to do, but I soon found otherwise. Holding objects with both hands is difficult — both to remember and to do. I'm a fan of multi-tasking and take pride in my ability to do several things at once. But when I was required to pass my purchase or my business card or my money with both hands, multi-tasking had to stop. Because my hands could hold only one thing, I was forced to give this action all of my attention.

This made me think about how I sometimes come to God with my 'hands' full of many things. I may put down whatever I'm grasping in one hand, but the other keeps clutching some worldly matter — dividing my attention and my heart. What I offer as worship comes from a distracted mind and heart, which, when I think about it, really isn't worship at all. To worship truly, I must come to God with my whole heart, offered with two hands.

Prayer: *Father, may we worship you with all that we are, and all our love. Amen.*

Thought for the Day: Today and every day, I will give God my full attention.

Dana Ryan (Arizona)

Stand Out

Read John 14:15-17, 25-26

Let your light shine before others, so that they may see your good works and give glory to your Father in heaven. Matthew 5:16 (NRSV)

Whenever I'm driving up the main road I always look to see if 'my' birch tree is still there. The tree is about 15 miles from my house, on the right side of the road. Its stark, white bark boldly stands out among the deep green leaves and brown bark of the other trees.

Like that birch tree, we are meant to stand out in this world, not to draw attention to ourselves but to draw attention to our Saviour. In a world full of darkness, people are searching for light. Where else are people going to see the light of Christ but in his followers?

Of course, God doesn't expect us to go out on our own. God equips us with the Holy Spirit and the Bible to guide us. The Bible teaches us that the world will know we are followers of Christ not because of any words we may say but because of the love we show to others. The love of God will make us shine like a birch among sycamores.

Prayer: *Father, give us the strength, the wisdom, and the love to shed your light in this dark world. In Jesus' name. Amen.*

Thought for the Day: How have you shown God's love today to others?

Travis Mamone (Maryland)

What Do These Stones Mean?

Read Psalm 102:1-7

When your children ask their parents in time to come, 'What do these stones mean?' then you shall let your children know, 'Israel crossed over the Jordan here on dry ground.' Joshua 4:21-22 (NRSV)

I am a cancer survivor. Last year I was diagnosed with Hodgkin's lymphoma, and I went through six months of gruelling chemotherapy. I am now in remission, and I am grateful each day for my family, my friends, my medical team and my God for their presence with me during my journey.

About halfway through my chemotherapy treatments, when I knew for certain how long they would last, I went to a nearby craftshop and bought a bag of coloured stones. I counted out one stone for each day from then until the day of my last chemo treatment. I put the jar of stones on the cupboard where I would see it frequently.

For the next three months, I ended each day by taking one stone out of the container, saying a prayer of thanksgiving, and putting the stone away in the drawer below. What did those stones mean to me? The jar of stones served as a visual reminder that my journey was, slowly but surely, coming to an end. It also helped me remember to thank God each day for the strength to get through that day, and to ask for the strength to get through the next one.

Prayer: *Loving God, thank you for your strength that gets us through each day. We are grateful for our families, our friends and our faith. Amen.*

Thought for the Day: What simple practice has helped you through a difficult time?

Lynne M. Deming (Tennessee)

PRAYER FOCUS: DOCTORS TREATING CANCER PATIENTS

Prayer Prompts

Read Psalm 25:4-10
Be joyful in hope, patient in affliction, faithful in prayer.
Romans 12:12 (NIV)

I put away my last Christmas decoration in late April. It was a crocheted bell-pull hanging on my bedroom door. The bell-pull was a gift from a beloved friend who was living with cancer. While Lynne struggled with the horrific effects of chemotherapy, she kept her mind and hands busy crocheting. I soon decided that every time I saw the bell-pull or heard its bells ring, I would pray for my friend.

After Christmas my friend was still ill, so I left the bell-pull on my door as a prayer prompt. Its gentle ringing was persistent in calling me to action. My friend is past the chemotherapy; her cancer is in remission now, and I give thanks for her recovery. But her gift became more than a Christmas decoration; it deepened my prayer life.

Now that the bell-pull is put away, I let other everyday sights and sounds nudge me into prayer. A loaf of bread reminds me to be thankful that my family can afford food. The newspaper encourages me to pray for the people and issues in the headlines. A candle's dancing flame is a cue to turn my thoughts to God, who lights my way. Finding God in the ordinary draws us closer to the heart of God.

Prayer: *Show us your ways, O Lord. Teach us how to draw nearer to you through frequent moments of prayer. Amen.*

Thought for the Day: Everyday objects and activities can call us to prayer.

Sherry Elliott (Tennessee)

Forgiving Others

Read Matthew 18:21-35

Be kind and compassionate to one another, forgiving each other, just as in Christ God forgave you. Ephesians 4:32 (NIV)

Sunday morning. Time for church. My husband collected our two older children and walked out of the door. I stayed behind, too hurt and angry to get myself and the baby ready to accompany him. I was reacting to a problem at church. I felt bitter and slighted. God knew I had a right to cry. I decided to stay at home and nurse my hurt feelings with angry tears.

As I was reaching for the baby's bottle, I heard a voice speak one word in my heart. 'Forgive.' I paused, startled. I knew whose voice I had heard. God was gently nudging me. It wasn't easy, but in time and with God's help I did forgive.

Now, at the age of 80, I look back to see how God has blessed and guided my life. In the past 50 years I have needed to heed that simple command again and again — 'Forgive!' Sometimes I delay and sometimes I complain, but, with God's help, I forgive. When I pray the Lord's Prayer, 'Forgive us our trespasses as we forgive those who trespass against us', I know what I must do. The peace and comfort of God's presence is worth the effort. We can forgive others with love because Christ first loved and forgave us.

Prayer: *Dear Lord, thank you for your word, the Bible, and for the words you speak in our hearts as we pray, 'Father, hallowed be your name, your kingdom come. Give us each day our daily bread. Forgive us our sins, for we also forgive everyone who sins against us. And lead us not into temptation.'* Amen.*

Thought for the Day: Whom do I need to forgive?

Joyce Woeste (Iowa)

*Luke 11:2-4 (NIV)

Do You Believe?

Read John 11:1-44

Jesus said to Martha, 'Those who believe in me, even though they die, will live, and everyone who lives and believes in me will never die. Do you believe this?' John 11:25-26 (NRSV)

To me, the raising of Lazarus is one of the most amazing of all the miracles Jesus performed. But there's a deeper insight in this story than the astonishing fact that he brought a dead man back to life. In our reading for today, Jesus says, 'Everyone who lives and believes in me will never die.' Then he asks Martha the ultimate question, 'Do you believe this?' The question may have been directed to Martha, but it is also a question that Jesus asks each of us: 'Do you believe?'

Though Jesus rescued his friend Lazarus from physical death once, ultimately Lazarus did die, as everyone does. But God rescues us from spiritual death, shows us the path to eternal life, and ends the separation between us.

If we come to believe in Jesus Christ as the Son of God, the resurrection and the life, then life triumphs over death. It sounds almost too easy, too good to be true: believe in Jesus, and have eternal life. But because of his death and resurrection, we can wrestle with the question and can come to believe.

Prayer: *Dear God, thank you for Jesus, who gave himself on the cross for us. Help us to extend your love to those who do not yet believe. Amen.*

Thought for the Day: What do you believe about Jesus?

John Bown (Minnesota)

Lean on God

Read 1 Kings 19:1-18

*[Elijah] prayed that he might die. 'I have had enough, LORD,' he said.
'Take my life.'* 1 Kings 19:4 (NIV)

I had lost my job. After a six-month search, I found work 2,500 miles
away. My wife and children stayed behind until we knew this job would
work out. My first three months alone were a nightmare. The new job
was challenging, and I missed my family. I felt alone and defeated, and
I cried in despair.

In times like this, I can really identify with Elijah. After he had been
empowered by God to resurrect a dead child, to stop the rain and to
bring fire down from heaven, Jezebel vowed to kill him. The fear and
pressure became too much for Elijah. When I see the great prophets in
despair and know the end of his story, I thank God because this means
there is hope for me. When pressures such as money problems, family
illness, stress at work or internal struggles make us feel defeated, we
can remember Elijah and how God tenderly cared for him.

One way to do this is to read the Bible daily so that we may become
encouraged and better tuned to God's voice. When we express our pain
in prayer and seek Christian companionship, God helps us through the
dark valley of depression. Elijah recovered and returned to serve God.
When we feel defeated, we too can lean on God and find hope.

Prayer: *Lord, help us to feel your presence when we're overwhelmed.
Amen.*

Thought for the Day: Though we may feel overwhelmed by our
problems, God is not overwhelmed.

Tom Smith (Utah)

Don't Turn Away

Read Mark 1:40-42

Jesus was filled with pity, and reached out and touched [the man with the skin disease]. Mark 1:41 (GNB)

When I was in my 30s I developed severe acne on my face, a disfigurement that was most embarrassing. My stepfather lived some distance from us, and a planned visit to his home coincided with a particularly bad outbreak of acne. What a mess I looked! I tapped the back door and warily walked in to greet him. Without a moment's hesitation, Andy affectionately kissed my cheek. How I loved him for that! Because of his tender gesture, I immediately felt affirmed and loved. My disfigurement didn't matter to Andy. He valued the real me, the inside person.

My stepfather's love challenges me to accept people who have blemishes of personality that make me want to turn away from them. My preference would be to smile quickly and steer past them, saying, 'Excuse me, but I just have to…'. But only by paying attention and listening to their story can I discover and value the inside person and offer the affirmation we all need.

Jesus set us an example when he touched and restored one of society's untouchables, 'a man suffering from a dreaded skin disease' (Mark 1:40). He did not act out of obligation or necessity, but in love and because he wanted to — just as Andy chose to kiss me.

Prayer: *God, may we gladly choose to act in love, reaching out to touch those who are suffering and shunned. Amen.*

Thought for the Day: Christ asks (and enables) us to love the unlovely.

Elaine Brown (Perthshire, Scotland)

Holy Conversation

Read James 3:1-10

What you say can preserve life or destroy it; so you must accept the consequences of your words. Proverbs 18:21 (GNB)

Improvising in a band is like having a conversation. When a band sounds good, each of the musicians is listening intently to the others in the group, carefully adding helpful musical phrases and building on the ideas of the other players. When a band sounds bad, that is akin to an argument. A soloist might play too long, exasperating the rest of the band; one member might fill the song with phrases that seem counter to the melody; musicians may drown each other out.

I am a musician. I also love to talk. I frequently find myself in conversations, and I am not always a good listener. Sometimes I am just as likely to play at the same time as the others in the band as I am to interrupt friends in conversation, attempting to replace their ideas with my own. Often when I play or speak impulsively, what comes out is sloppy, confusing or wrong. God has used Proverbs 18:21 to remind me to watch my words: 'What you say can preserve life or destroy it.'

I am sobered by realising the power of the tongue. Just as listening to the music of the band, building on their ideas rather than forcing my own, will bear musical fruit, so listening and thinking before I speak can contribute to helpful conversations.

Prayer: *Creator God, help us to speak as you want us to speak today, that all our conversations may be holy conversations. Amen.*

Thought for the Day: There is power in what you say; speak carefully.

Andrew Rogers (Michigan)

True Worth

Read Isaiah 43:1-7

When they call to me, I will answer them; I will be with them in trouble, I will rescue them and honour them. Psalm 91:15 (NRSV)

'What could you do with £20?" asked our minister during children's time in the church service. The kids jumped with grasping hands as he waved the note in front of them. Then, to their consternation, he crumpled it up and threatened to deface it or even tear it. Finally, he pointed out to them that no matter what he did to it, it would still be worth £20.

And so it is with human life. Terrorist attacks, global-economic collapse, natural disasters, accidents, illness and other losses can threaten to crush us, deface us and tear us to shreds. But can the worst events that we encounter ever destroy our value? After all, whose are we? The LORD says, 'I have called you by name, you are mine' (Isa. 43:1, NRSV). The apostle Paul stressed that nothing 'will be able to separate us from the love of God in Christ Jesus our Lord' (Rom. 8:39, NRSV).

The Bible is telling us that whatever happens, even when the worst has been done, the last word still belongs to God. Nothing that happens can diminish our worth to a God who holds, sustains and cherishes us.

Prayer: *Dear God, we praise you for giving us lives of meaning and purpose whose value can never be destroyed by tragic events. Amen.*

Thought for the Day: Thanks be to God who gives us victory in Christ Jesus our Lord!

John Franklin (Manawatu-Wanganui region, New Zealand)

Not Ashamed

Read 2 Timothy 1:3-14

God did not give us a spirit of cowardice, but rather a spirit of power and of love and of self-discipline. 2 Timothy 1:7 (NRSV)

I work in education, where I sometimes find it intimidating openly to express my Christian beliefs. Recently, a colleague told me about some health problems his daughter was experiencing. Instead of telling this man that I would pray for his daughter, I told him I would 'think a good thought'.

That evening at home, as I remembered what I'd said, I felt ashamed of not expressing my faith. I knew that my shallow words grieved God.

The following day, I went back and told my colleague that I was sorry for not saying what I'd really wanted to say, that I would pray for his daughter. To my surprise the man smiled and then hugged me, telling me that he too was a believer!

What a blessing I would have missed had I not confessed my beliefs! Now I not only have the joy of fellowship with another believer; I also know the peace of having taken a stand for my faith.

Prayer: *Heavenly Father, give us the courage to speak about our faith in you today. In Jesus' name we pray. Amen.*

Thought for the Day: Am I shaping or being shaped by my world?

Linda M. Wall (Oregon)

Longings Fulfilled

Read 1 Samuel 1:21-28

Hope deferred makes the heart sick, but a longing fulfilled is a tree of life.
Proverbs 13:12 (NIV)

As I sat in the obstetrician's office, I felt heartbroken. For the second time, my husband and I had lost a baby through miscarriage. Our hope of starting a family was deferred again. Less than a year later, however, I was overjoyed when God fulfilled my longing and gave us a son.

Recently, I read 1 Samuel 1. I identified with Hannah's desire to have children. Pouring out her heart to the Lord, she prayed for years that God would bless her with a son and vowed to dedicate him to the Lord. She eventually conceived and gave birth to a son, Samuel. 'I prayed for this child,' she said, 'and the Lord has granted me what I asked of him. So now I give him to the Lord' (1 Sam. 1:27-28, NIV).

Reading Hannah's story reminded me to recognise my child as a gift that I should continually surrender to the Lord. It would have been easy for Hannah to keep Samuel to herself after years of hoping for a child. But she offered him back, in thanksgiving and praise, to serve the Lord.

Indeed, all of our fulfilled hopes are gifts from God and reminders that all we have comes from, and belongs to, the Lord. Our proper response to God is gratitude and surrender.

Prayer: *Thank you, God, for prayers you have answered and longings you have fulfilled. Help us to remember your grace and faithfulness and to respond to your blessings by making them an offering of love to you. Amen.*

Thought for the Day: Every fulfilled hope is a gift from God.

Kelley Brown (Alabama)

Personal Best

Read Matthew 22:34-40

Let us run with perseverance the race that is set before us, looking to Jesus the pioneer and perfecter of our faith. Hebrews 12:1-2 (NRSV)

On my first day on a swimming team, I was 11 years old and thought I was a pretty good swimmer. Actually, I wasn't a great competitor at first, but I loved records; I made it my goal always to break my own. Sometimes I would be the last one to finish in a race, but I would jump out of the water and run excitedly to my coach and say, 'Hey, coach, I beat my best time!'

My performance improved, and later I won the district competition in the 100-yard breaststroke when I was at high school. But the best part about that race was that I beat my previous best time. This way of thinking became part of my personality, and it became part of my faith too.

In Matthew 22:34-40 Jesus taught the greatest commandment, but keeping it sounds difficult, almost impossible. Still, I've learned from swimming that we don't reach our goal on the first day of practice. Learning to love God and our neighbour takes a lot of persistence, and we will face many setbacks. It is easier to love others when we're not worried about who is winning and who is losing, who is better and who is worse. Instead, we can find ways to celebrate our gifts together. And though we will not become saints overnight, we can do a little better each day. I'm not yet what God wants me to be, but thank God I'm better than I used to be.

Prayer: *Lord God, strengthen our faith as we exercise it. Teach us persistence in our love for others. In Jesus' name we pray. Amen.*

Thought for the Day: Practice makes better.

David Turner (Texas)

PRAYER FOCUS: ATHLETES IN COMPETITIONS

Into the Light

Read John 12:37-46

You are a chosen people, a royal priesthood, a holy nation, a people belonging to God, that you may declare the praises of him who called you out of darkness into his wonderful light. 1 Peter 2:9 (NIV)

I couldn't believe it — a flower bud! I had purchased the amaryllis 18 months before. The directions on the box said to keep the bulb cool and dry for three months after the plant finished blooming. So, after the flowers died, I took the pot to the basement and forgot about it.

Before going on holiday, I carried the neglected bulb outside. Daylight and whatever rain fell during those three weeks energised the dormant amaryllis. When I moved it inside, it produced a 22-inch stem topped with three elegant, pink-veined flowers. And what made the difference? It came out of darkness into light.

Jesus said, 'I have come into the world as a light, so that no one who believes in me should stay in darkness'(John 12:46, NIV). God's word nurtures us and helps us to mature into strong followers of Christ. If we are willing to follow the Holy Spirit's guidance daily, others will see God's goodness in us. They can see our hope, courage, comfort, peace and joy. In both bright times and seasons of darkness, we can glorify the One who brought us into the marvellous light of Christ.

Prayer: *Father, may my life bring you glory and show others what a joy it is to serve you. Amen.*

Thought for the Day: We are meant to shine with God's light.

Mary Waind (Ontario, Canada)

My Bible

Read 1 Timothy 4:11-16

Continue in what you have learned and have become convinced of, because you know those from whom you learned it, and how from infancy you have known the holy Scriptures. 2 Timothy 3:14-15 (NIV)

I am the proud owner of an antique medical book, *The Practice of Surgery*. It was written by Sir Ashley Cooper, 'Surgeon to the King', and published in 1828. The book was a gift from a close friend, and I keep it in a prominent place in my office. I make sure it is easily visible for people to see when they visit me. I don't often read it, and I certainly don't follow its recommendations in my practice of medicine! It is out of date; I keep it only for show.

Many of us treat our Bible in the same way. Though the Bible may be the greatest bestseller of all time, it is perhaps the least read book on our shelf. We like to display our Bible in a prominent place, but we don't necessarily follow its recommendations. Many people feel it is out of date. The Bible was written by human hands but under the inspiration of God. It proclaims eternal truths. When we read the Bible, God will speak to us through its pages — as to countless others before us.

Prayer: *Lord, help us to read the Bible daily, discovering food for our soul and guidance for our spiritual journey. Amen.*

Thought for the Day: The truths of the Bible are never out of date.

Bill Scurlock (Arkansas)

PRAYER FOCUS: PHYSICIANS

Choosing Friends

Read 1 Corinthians 13
Do not be misled: 'Bad company corrupts good character.'
1 Corinthians 15:33 (NIV)

As parents, my husband and I stress to our children the importance of choosing godly friends. We urge them to choose friends who are willing to share in their joys as well as in their struggles. We want them to have steadfast friends — people they know they can count on, no matter what happens.

It is important for all of us to choose godly friends, friends who uplift and encourage us. However, we also need friends who are not afraid to let us know when we begin to stray from the ways of God and lovingly guide us back to the right path.

I have been blessed with such a friend. When I need someone to pray with me or just listen to my joys and sorrows, she is the one I telephone. I often turn to her for her wise and godly guidance. I can count on her to encourage me, but I also know that she will gently nudge me back on course if necessary. The true friends we want for ourselves and our children demonstrate these qualities of love as well as those mentioned in 1 Corinthians 13.

We have no friend greater than Christ. However, God also places godly people in our path to befriend us. We can be thankful for them and their influence on our lives. In turn, it is also our privilege as followers of Christ to be that same kind of friend to others.

Prayer: *Father, thank you for sending us godly friends. Help us to be godly friends to others. Thank you for Jesus, our truest friend. Amen.*

Thought for the Day: God brings people into our lives to bring us closer to Christ.

Marcia Hodge (Florida)

Just Me

Read Romans 12:1-8
For God alone my soul waits in silence; from him comes my salvation.
Psalm 62:1 (NRSV)

When I was younger, I thought it was necessary to have an important role in life so that people would love me. I always tried to look my best, spending hours on my external appearance. I longed to be accepted by every group I came into contact with — other students and people at social gatherings. Yet it seemed difficult to please those around me despite my tremendous efforts. As a result, I felt more and more self-conscious, shy and unaccepted. I desperately wanted signs from others to show that they considered me somebody important.

But while studying the Bible, I discovered God's way of measuring myself. As I sought first to do God's will, I became less self-conscious. Over the years I've gained more self-assurance. This seemed to happen in a natural way, just as I was changing my priorities. And instead of seeking approval from others, I slowly learned to extend the love and acceptance of Christ. Consequently, I became more relaxed and I no longer worried about my image or status. Transformed by the love of Christ, I've made many friends just by being myself.

Prayer: *Loving God, help us to rely on you for a sense of purpose and reassurance as we live each day. In Jesus' name. Amen.*

Thought for the Day: We witness best by being who God created us to be.

Helgard Maria Zotter (Geneva, Switzerland)

PRAYER FOCUS: THOSE WHO LONG TO BE IMPORTANT

God's Gift of Prayer

Read Philippians 4:4-9

Do not be anxious about anything, but in everything, by prayer and petition, with thanksgiving, present your requests to God.
Philippians 4:6 (NIV)

I am 85, and my heart functions at 20 per cent of normal capacity. I am weak and have little energy; I feel that I will be with Jesus soon. Because of my condition, I think about many things, especially about my relationship with God, and I pray a lot.

Prayer is a powerful gift, and yet we often fail to use it. We let other priorities crowd out time with our Creator. What a salute to God when we, together with thousands of others, give thanks for the life given to us. We are thankful for God's love, God's spirit, God's healing hand, God's guiding light and God's comforting grace.

We can see love and goodness when we are in close relationship with God and are following the words and doing the works recommended by Jesus. What a blessing God has given to us: the opportunity to pray.

Prayer: *Dear God, open our hearts and minds to hear your call. Nurture our relationship with you as we pray the way Jesus taught us, saying, 'Our Father which art in heaven, Hallowed be thy name. Thy kingdom come. Thy will be done, as in heaven, so in earth. Give us day by day our daily bread. And forgive us our sins; for we also forgive every one that is indebted to us. And lead us not into temptation; but deliver us from evil.'* Amen.*

Thought for the Day: God longs for time with each of us.

James H. Norman (Texas)

*Luke 11:2-4 (KJV)

Gifts and Talents

Read 1 Peter 4:10-11
Serve one another with whatever gift each of you has received.
1 Peter 4:10 (NRSV)

Why me? Why was she sure that I would agree to lead a discussion group? Did the leader of the women's society know that I had a gift that would be of service to the group?

Although I had served as a children's Sunday School teacher, I had never led other kinds of groups in the church. This would be a challenge. I agreed to lead the group, and then I prayed, fasted, studied and prepared the material for the session.

By observing the active group's participation and response, I both enjoyed and learned from the experience. God was surely in our midst. I was thankful and pleased to have done this task.

I thought about how many times we could help others by sharing the gifts and knowledge God has given us, but we have not done so. Why? God can bless others if we try to learn, understand, obey and follow God's will. As we share experiences and knowledge, we will grow ourselves and help others to grow, too.

Prayer: *Lord, instil in us the desire to praise your name by sharing and using the gifts and talents you have given us. Amen.*

Thought for the Day: What gifts and talents can I use to help God's people?

Norma L. Santos (Puerto Rico)

PRAYER FOCUS: TO BE GOOD STEWARDS OF OUR GIFTS

Eager Efforts

Read Ephesians 2:1-10
We are what he has made us, created in Christ Jesus for good works.
Ephesians 2:10 (NRSV)

One spring my wife and I planted gardenias. 'We'll help,' said our two young sons. We gave them trowels, and they began digging. Before we knew it, they were off playing with their toys, leaving a few shallow holes in the dirt. Of course we didn't mind. Actually, we were pleased by their effort.

But if I'd hired a landscaping firm to plant those gardenias, I'd have been upset. 'You won't get paid until it's done right,' I might have said. That thought reminded me of the difference between serving as a response to God's grace and love and serving in an attempt to earn these with our works. It's the difference between the eager offerings that children give their parents and the anxious toil that workers may do for their employer.

Our position in our Father's house is secure. Even if our good works are mixed with the remnants of sin and the best we can do is to dig shallow holes for the Almighty, God is pleased with our effort. When we look for salvation in God's grace and not in our own good deeds, we are free to offer joyful service.

Prayer: *Dear Father, help us to remember that we are not your employees but your children. As such, we long to be like you and to serve you. Amen.*

Thought for the Day: Good works are the effect, not the cause, of our salvation.

Marvin Lindsay (Virginia)

Relentless for Justice

Read Luke 18:1-8

Will not God grant justice to his chosen ones who cry to him day and night? Will he delay long in helping them? I tell you, he will quickly grant justice to them. Luke 18:7-8 (NRSV)

In the parable of the widow and the unjust judge, we meet an extraordinary woman who refuses to accept her fate. She voices opposition to injustice without relenting. As a result of her persistence, even the unjust judge is prompted to act.

If even an unjust judge can be moved to grant justice, then imagine how much God desires to help those who are wronged. God looks upon the foreigner, the orphan and the widow with deep concern for their plight. With our help, God can respond. The image of God wanting justice for them gives me hope as I think of Darfur, Sudan, where more than 300,000 people have died over the past three years as a result of civil unrest, lack of food and disease. It is probably the worst humanitarian crisis in the world today.

While I am easily overwhelmed and feel discouraged, I draw strength from our God who does not forget Darfur. The cries of people around the world do not go unheard. I pray that Christians will pray unrelentingly, demonstrate and call for peace with justice on behalf of our brothers and sisters everywhere.

Prayer: *God our Judge, give us determination and courage relentlessly to seek and work for justice on behalf of our neighbours. Amen.*

Thought for the Day: We serve God when we work for justice.

David Wesley Poe (Missouri)

PRAYER FOCUS: THE PEOPLE OF DARFUR, SUDAN

Tithing

Read Malachi 3:6-12

Honour the LORD with your substance and with the first fruits of all your produce; then your barns will be filled with plenty.
Proverbs 3:9-10 (NRSV)

For years I struggled with the concept of tithing. I didn't mind putting a little in the offering plate each Sunday, but 10 per cent? I dreamed up lots of reasons why I couldn't tithe, yet I had no trouble spending the same amount at the shops.

Then I met Anne, a single woman who not only tithed but saved as much as she could for missions. Anne had a joy and a confidence in God that I envied. She didn't have a high-paying job, yet she lived in style and within her means. One day, I asked for her secret. 'I follow God's plan and trust him,' she confided. She went on to explain that tithing isn't an obligation but a privilege and a way of showing that we honour God. 'God has never let me down, even during the hardest of times,' Anne said.

God challenged me through Anne. 'Test me in this,' God seemed to say. So I took God up on it and have never looked back. God has faithfully kept the assurances given in the Bible, and blessings flow out to me day by day. Because God is faithful and generous, I always have enough.

Prayer: *Dear God, help us to believe in your word and put it to work in our life. Amen.*

Thought for the Day: We can never out-give God.

Karen Gallagher (Florida)

Growing

Read Psalm 119:9-16

One does not live by bread alone, but by every word that comes from the mouth of the LORD. Deuteronomy 8:3 (NRSV)

Occasionally, a mother sheep in our flock dies or suffers ill-health during lambing. When we have orphan lambs to raise, we feed them regularly with bottled milk formulated for lambs. After two or three days, they learn to recognise that our arrival means food. Before long, they greet us with great enthusiasm. They butt and shove one another, competing to be first to be satisfied with a good supply of warm, nutritious milk.

The lambs' enthusiasm for their life-giving sustenance causes me to consider our attitudes toward God's word. Do we thirst to learn more about God, eagerly anticipating the lessons and blessings in the Bible? Do we regard it as life-giving, enabling us to grow in our faith and to develop spiritually as we should? The words and promises in the Bible strengthen us through difficulties and teach us how to live our daily lives. But more important, studying scripture helps to lead us to a closer, growing relationship with God.

Prayer: *Heavenly Father, make us eager to feed on your word and spend time with you every day. In Jesus' name we pray. Amen.*

Thought for the Day: Time with God is the most worthwhile time of all.

Ann Sloane (New South Wales, Australia)

A Hardened Heart

Read Mark 8:14-21
I will remove from them their heart of stone and give them a heart of flesh. Ezekiel 11:19 (NIV)

While watching a television documentary, I learned that heart rhythm problems in some cases can be caused by dead heart cells. Heart cells can die from internal as well as external causes. The dead cells do not conduct electrical impulses along the correct, predetermined path.

Likewise, the spiritual heart can be impaired. If we allow it, emotional injuries and our own behaviour can harden our spiritual heart over time. The callous remarks we sometimes make to others can hurt them and cause them to harden their hearts as well. A hardened heart is spiritually impaired and doesn't work as it was designed to. Jesus implied that a hardened heart impedes faith, discernment and understanding.

As far as I know, dead cells in a physical heart cannot be revived. But this is not true for our spiritual heart. God's grace creates in us a clean, new and perfect heart when we recognise our need and call on the Lord.

Prayer: *Dear God, soften my heart where hardness impairs my relationship with you and my neighbours. Restore in me a healthy spiritual heart. Amen.*

Thought for the Day: God offers each of us a new heart.

Kenneth Athon (Indiana)

Letting Go

Read 1 Thessalonians 5:12-18
Give thanks in all circumstances; for this is the will of God in Christ Jesus for you. 1 Thessalonians 5:18 (NRSV)

I knocked on the door, but no one answered. 'June, are you here?' I called out as I walked into the bedroom. I had come to take my mother-in-law to her doctor's appointment; instead, I found her unconscious on the floor. Four days later she died.

For months as I grieved her passing, I replayed the events of her last days. As her carer, I asked myself, Could I have done more? June had been difficult to get along with, and at times I resented her dependence on me. But through prayer and meditation I eventually made peace with her death. I came to understand that it had been an honour to serve her and that I had made her last months more bearable. From my life with June I learned patience and compassion.

I no longer question what happened that day but rather thank God for time spent with her. It is easy to thank God for the good things in life, but real growth comes when we are able to thank God for our difficulties.

Prayer: *Thank you, God, for placing in our lives people who need our love — and for reminding us that our purpose in life is to serve you by serving others. Amen.*

Thought for the Day: In everything give thanks to God.

Margaret Norton (Missouri)

PRAYER FOCUS: THOSE CARING FOR ELDERLY RELATIVES

A Kinder, Gentler God

Read 1 John 4:13-21

Love is made complete among us so that we will have confidence on the day of judgment… There is no fear in love. But perfect love drives out fear, because fear has to do with punishment. The one who fears is not made perfect in love. 1 John 4:17-18 (NIV)

When I was growing up, my family seldom attended church. Out of curiosity, I would sometimes listen to preaching on the radio. Most of these preachers seemed to say that we should live in constant fear that we might go to hell. When I began to attend church on my own, I was surprised that I heard much more about God's love than about hell. Sin was never discussed without mention of forgiveness. I liked this kinder, gentler God, but I still worried: Is this church watering down the Gospel? Aren't we supposed to fear God's punishment?

Then one day I read the passage above from 1 John. I was so relieved to read that fear of being punished by God is not a sign of a great faith but of incomplete or imperfect faith. As the writer of Hebrews 10:22-23 expressed it, we can, 'draw near to God with a sincere heart in full assurance of faith… Let us hold unswervingly to the hope we profess, for he who promised is faithful' (NIV).

I have learned that the biblical meaning of 'fearing' is having a great awe and reverence. It does not mean living in terror of Judgement Day.

Prayer: *Loving God, help us always to sense your love for us and peace as we seek a closer relationship with you. Amen.*

Thought for the Day: 'Fear of God' is awe, not terror.

Michael A. Macdonald (North Carolina)

Blind Dependence

Read Matthew 20:29-34

Jesus had compassion on [the two blind men] and touched their eyes.
Matthew 20:34 (NIV)

Last summer while training to be a counsellor, I had to go rock climbing — blindfolded. The height alone petrified me, but the thought of attempting to climb without being able to see turned my stomach into cement. I felt desperate and was utterly dependent on the others. I slipped. Reaching up, I couldn't grasp the next handhold. Dangling blind from the side of a cliff, I didn't care if people knew that I was vulnerable and couldn't cope alone. I was about to fall. Then I heard the deep, confident voice of my teammate cutting through my fear, giving me the directions I needed to find the handhold.

Much like me in my situation, the only thing that the two blind men on the road to Jericho could 'see' was their problem, their helplessness. Desperate, they only shouted louder when the crowd tried to quiet them. Just as I had to tune out everything but my teammate's voice, the blind men had to focus on Jesus and not let the condemning voices or their helpless state deter them.

When the blind men ignored the crowd and focused on Jesus he heard and responded. Their turning to him in complete vulnerability freed God to work. In the same way, when we call out in our need, just as Jesus came to the blind men on the roadside, God will hear us and respond to our cry.

Prayer: *Dear God, help us to see our weakness, to focus on your voice above the crowd, and to completely depend on you. Amen.*

Thought for the Day: Where do I cry out for God's help?

Rosemarie Greenawalt (Pest, Hungary)

PRAYER FOCUS: THOSE IN JOB TRAINING

God's Time

Read Psalm 37
Commit your way to the Lord; trust in him, and he will act.
Psalm 37:5 (NRSV)

One day, I learned an important lesson about making a cake. When I had combined all the ingredients, I poured the mixture into the baking tin and put it in the oven. After 40 minutes, the cake smelled so good that I could not help peeking through the oven's glass window. I saw that the cake had risen and looked ready. So I turned off the oven and took out the cake. I called my mother, showed her the cake, and asked her to taste it. However, when she cut into the cake she found out that the middle wasn't completely cooked. She told me that I should have baked the cake for another five minutes.

This experience reminded me of how impatient we are in waiting for God's answers to our prayers. My impatience in taking out the cake is like our impatient attitude towards God. We often want a 'quick fix' from God when a hasty response might make matters worse. Often I have to be reminded that our God is an 'on-time God' — neither too late nor too early to help. We can trust that God wants the best for us and that we will see God's glory at last.

Prayer: *Dear Lord, forgive our impatience. Remind us that our time is not your time and that you always desire the best for us. Amen.*

Thought for the Day: God's timing is different — and better — than ours.

Marcelina Dewi Kumalasari (Jakarta Barat, Indonesia)

Raccoons at the Table

Read Philippians 1:15-18

What does it matter? The important thing is that in every way, whether from false motives or true, Christ is preached. And because of this I rejoice.
Philippians 1:18 (NIV)

One night while we were camping, raccoons tore into a bag of rubbish I had neglected to hang up out of reach. I rose early and found myself in the midst of a mess, pondering three simple thoughts. First, 'This is what raccoons do.' Second, 'They really didn't hurt me.' Third, 'Next time, I'll tie my rubbish up higher!'

God led me to write in my journal about the 'raccoons' in my life, people who seemed to go through my 'rubbish' — my weaknesses, scars and unresolved pain — making a mess and causing me problems. One by one, I prayed for and about them, remembering the three thoughts above.

In Philippians, Paul spoke of those who 'preached Christ out of selfish ambition, not sincerely, supposing they could stir up trouble' for him while he was in prison. But Paul had learned to let go of anger at people like this. He said, 'What does it matter?' (NIV).

There are people in our lives who seem to rummage through our weaknesses, trying to 'stir up trouble'. But anger, retaliation and distress are unnecessary. As Jesus told his disciples, we can be 'wise as serpents' and 'harmless as doves' (Matt. 10:16, KJV). All of us, even troublemakers, are welcome at God's table.

Prayer: *Lord, help us to face life's troublemakers with confidence in your power to help us. Fill us with the light of understanding. In Christ's name. Amen.*

Thought for the Day: Troublemakers are troubled people. Pray for them!
Stephen P. West (Alabama)

Making Prayer Visible

Almost every morning and evening on the bus or train, commuters discuss people or events they've heard about in news reports, the newspaper, or conversation. Queuing at the supermarket or waiting in a doctor's surgery, we often hear people doing the same. Many such exchanges end with someone saying something like, 'But there's nothing we can do about it' or 'Somebody ought to do something!'

Believers can always do something: we can pray. Many times, however, we do not see praying as doing something. With our culture's emphasis on doing, producing and achieving, we can easily dismiss prayer because it does not result in a product. Perhaps finding ways to make our praying more visible, making prayer more than 'just words' can help us to be more faithful.

Here are some strategies to make our praying more visible. Consider how your life of prayer could be enriched by trying one or more of these:

1. Establish a regular place to pray — a personal holy space. On a small table beside my bedroom chair, I have placed a candle, a cross and several other items that hold special meaning for me — including a small china box that reminds me of my church, the community of faith that formed me. When I sit in that chair, my mind and my spirit know why I am there; pattern and familiarity make paying attention to God seem right and comfortable.

2. Keep a prayer list. Write in a notebook or journal the names of people and situations that you want to bring before God. Refer to the list every week or so and give thanks for how God has been at work in these matters.

3. Make your monthly calendar into a call to prayer. Write the names of those you want to pray for on the day of each month that corresponds to their birthday. From time to time, send a note to the ones you are praying for, letting them know you have their names before you to remind you to bring them before God.

4. Prayer map (1): Make a 'prayer map' of your neighbourhood, with blocks to represent each home. Write in the names of your neighbours and their needs. During your prayer time, work your way around the neighbourhood, praying for people by name. If you don't know your neighbours, ask God to help you find ways to reach out to them. Update the map as you progress in building relationships, making friends with your neighbours to help them become friends of Christ.

5. Prayer map (2): Place a map of the world or a small globe where you can see it as you pray. (If you have children in your home, you might use a world-map area rug to help them intercede for the world's needs as a part of bedtime prayer, directing them to stand on a different continent each day of the week.) Hold the map or globe and picture God lovingly reaching out to each area where there is trouble. Consider how God wants you to respond to the needs that come to mind.

6. 'Pray the news'. Each day as you listen to or read news reports, list the people and problems mentioned. Spend time sitting quietly with God, holding the list in your hands. Offer the needs represented by the list to God, waiting to see how God may nudge you to respond.

We can also make our prayers more than 'just words' by combining prayer with action. Here are some possibilities:

1. Prayer walking. Walk regularly through your neighbourhood or work area with the intention to notice people and needs, praying for them as you walk. Use cues — toys outside, pictures on desks — to suggest how you might pray.

2. A prayer shawl ministry. People in these ministries knit or crochet covers to be given to those in special need. While working, the one doing needlework prays for the person who will receive the prayer shawl. (Visit www.shawlministry.com for more information.) In my church, our prayer shawl ministry gives these to people who are grieving or undergoing medical treatment, as a sign of our congregation's presence with them and prayers for them. A prayer shawl is a sort of visible hug that can comfort.

3. Find an activity that helps you focus your attention on God. This might be gardening, painting, writing in a journal, running. Some people find that moving or keeping physically busy allows them to put aside distractions that interfere when they try simply to sit quietly and pray. Colossians 3:17 tells us to do all that we do as 'unto the Lord', turning all our actions into prayer.

Mary Lou Redding

Come to the Water

Read John 4:1-15

Come, all you who are thirsty, come to the waters. Isaiah 55:1 (NIV)

Our home, the Canary Island of Lanzarote 60 miles off the coast of Morocco, receives little rainfall. Water is precious since it comes from the sea and has to be desalinated for our use. As a result, the island has a desert look. This makes tending and watering the thirsty flowers of our small garden even more important to me. Like the garden, we island residents often get thirsty and need to drink plenty of water.

Water is also very important in the story of the Samaritan woman at the well. Here, Jesus tells her — and us — that he can satisfy our spiritual thirst. He is able to refresh us with Living Water from an eternal source. What a blessing this is when we are spiritually dry!

When we feel parched and barren, Christ stretches out his arms to welcome us into a fountain of blessing. His living water abounds to refresh our souls. We don't have to wait until we are dehydrated; we can come to Christ to be refreshed.

Prayer: *Living Water, wash over us and fill us. Satisfy our thirst for you. Amen.*

Thought for the Day: Living Water can quench our thirst.

Jo Sherard (Lanzarote, Spain)

The Daily Devotional Guide

Read 1 Corinthians 15:50-58

Death has been swallowed up in victory. 1 Corinthians 15:54 (NRSV)

It's Thursday morning. I stand and stare. The bed is empty. A simple metal frame is all that remains, stripped of mattress, sheets and pillows. The rude truth strikes me that my mother, who spent almost five years in this bed, is dead. I gaze at the empty bed. Then my eyes move to the bedside table. My mother's copy of *The Upper Room* daily devotional guide rests on top of her Bible — a timely reminder of the healing power of spending time with God each day. I leave the room to take care of her funeral arrangements.

A few days later I return to share the gist of Mother's funeral service with Paula and Joy, the other two bedridden occupants of the room. To my surprise, someone new occupies my mother's bed. She smiles at me as she puts down Mother's copy of *The Upper Room*. 'I have been reading this little book since I got here on Friday,' she says. 'It helps me a lot each day.'

As I leave I ponder. After five years of travel every other weekend, I'll not need to return here again. But maybe I will. How else will the occupants of that bed get their copies of *The Upper Room*?

Death is not the end — for Mother or for me. It's simply the beginning of a new journey, another day serving the Lord.

Prayer: *Thank you, God, for offering us your peace even in times of sorrow. Thank you for giving us new life, both here and in eternity. Amen.*

Thought for the Day: Death is not the end — just another beginning.

Roland Rink (Gauteng, South Africa)

Light in the Darkness

Read Isaiah 60:1-3
You are the light of the world. A city built on a hill cannot be hid.
Matthew 5:14 (NRSV)

Each summer, my family and I travel to a retreat centre on an island off the coast of New Hampshire. Every evening, we worship in a tiny stone chapel perched on a rise at the centre of the island. We gather in silence at the base of the hill, listening to the deep tolling of the bell that calls us to worship. Each person carries a candle lantern to the chapel, which has no electricity. As we venture up the narrow, rocky path, we hear the cries of seagulls, the crash of waves and the whistle of wind on the water.

As one person after another climbs the hill, a line of candlelight gradually lengthens and grows, wavering in the darkness. The chapel begins to glow brighter as people enter and hang up their lanterns.

When I see a candle or a lantern, I remember that Jesus came to be the light of the world. Each of us carries God's light within us and can shine that light for others. We are beacons, inviting others to follow Jesus and to answer God's invitation to new life.

Prayer: *Illuminating God, let your light shine through us so that others may clearly see and follow you. Amen.*

Thought for the Day: We are God's light, shining to show the way to life.

Susan J. Foster (Connecticut)

In the Garden

Read 1 Samuel 3:1-10

'Be still, and know that I am God! I am exalted among the nations, I am exalted in the earth.' Psalm 46:10 (NRSV)

I love noise — not loud, blaring noise, but steady, constant reminders that I am not alone in this world. Radio, television, the sound of other family members clanking around in the kitchen — all of these are a joy to me. And when no one else is around to make noise for me, I create the illusion of company by making noise myself. This need for company even carries over to my relationship with God. More often than not, when I've run out of things to say, I start saying the same things over again just to 'keep the dialogue going'.

Unfortunately, while I am busy talking, no one else is able to. Over the years, I have discovered that God is a very polite listener and refuses to talk when I am talking. God consistently waits to speak until I'm ready to hear it.

Finally, knowing this day might never come, God gently began nudging me towards the hobby of gardening — an activity that occupies me so well I didn't think about talking. Amazingly, as I pull the weeds out of the dirt to make room for my herbs and vegetables and flowers, I am silent. I hear the birds and feel the wind, but I am content with no need to comment. Thoughts about my day, my friends, family and colleagues simply drift away, and I am with God. For me, time in the garden is prayer.

Prayer: *Lord, help us always to find a setting where we can listen to you. Calm us to hear your quiet whisper. Amen.*

Thought for the Day: God waits for us in the silence.

Anna C. Gheen (Idaho)

Barabbas

Read Romans 14:1-12

God, who is rich in mercy, made us alive with Christ even when we were dead in transgressions. Ephesians 2:4-5 (NIV)

Not much is revealed in the Bible about Barabbas except that he was a criminal being held under sentence of death for insurrection and murder. After Jesus' trial, Pilate released Barabbas and sent Jesus to be crucified. How strange that a criminal should be set free and the sinless, spotless, perfect Son of God should die in his place! In films about the Easter story, Barabbas is portrayed as a detestable character; he is not the sort of person that anyone would die to save. But that is exactly what Jesus did.

When I am tempted to look down on people as unworthy of salvation, I remember that Jesus died to save Barabbas just as he died for me — and everyone else in the world. God loves everyone equally, and Jesus died for the sins of each of us, without exception. In the sight of God, everyone has equal access to the gift of salvation through Jesus Christ our Lord.

Prayer: *Thank you, God, for the gift of salvation. Help us to see others with your eyes of love. Amen.*

Thought for the Day: No matter who I am or what I have done, God loves me.

Richard Wiseman (Ohio)

PRAYER FOCUS: THOSE WHO DON'T KNOW ABOUT SALVATION

A Faithful Witness

Read Isaiah 12:1-6

The joy of the LORD is your strength. Nehemiah 8:10 (NRSV)

Martha, our sister in the Lord, was in hospital because she had sustained a very serious fracture. The prognosis was not good. In all probability she would never walk again.

I went with the youth group to visit her in the hospital. We began to talk to her, but instead of our group offering words of hope and encouragement to her, she shared a vision of faith and words of strength with us. When I returned home, I recalled the words that had affected me the most: 'The joy of the Lord is our strength. We must remain faithful to God at all times.'

Martha has died, but time has not erased the memory of her faithful witness and her trust in God under difficult circumstances. Now, I don't dwell on how big my problems are; rather, I remember how great my God is.

Prayer: *Faithful God, in the midst of our problems, help us to see your power. As Jesus taught us, we pray, 'Our Father in heaven, hallowed be your name, your kingdom come, your will be done on earth as it is in heaven. Give us today our daily bread. Forgive us our debts, as we also have forgiven our debtors. And lead us not into temptation, but deliver us from the evil one.'* Amen.*

Thought for the Day: Even in difficult times, we can witness to God's goodness.

Roberto Herrera (Holguin, Cuba)

*Matthew 6:9-13 (NIV)

Pretentious or Plain?

Read Jeremiah 18:1-10

You turn things upside down, as if the potter were thought to be like the clay! Shall what is formed say to him who formed it, 'He did not make me'? Can the pot say of the potter, 'He knows nothing'?
Isaiah 29:16 (NIV)

I have to admit that I have trouble with the concept of being clay and not having a voice in my development. It's not that I'm rebellious and want my own way; it's just that I want some say in what happens to me. Okay, I admit it. I'm afraid that God's plan for me won't suit mine. What if I would make a great ceramic bowl to be displayed and admired but instead I get made into an ashtray? All right, maybe being a display bowl is too pretentious. But what if I would make a great serving dish that could be useful in many ways, but I get made into a chamber pot? (In that case, I think I'd rather be an ashtray.)

In my mind, I know that God wants not only what is good for me but also what is best for me. Still, I have trouble feeling that in my heart and living it in my life, especially when people around me treat me as if I am an ashtray or worse.

I've learned that when I do what God wants us to do, I am being who God wants us to be. I won't have to worry about how that might look to me or to anyone else.

Prayer: *Father, help us to be who you want us to be, where you put us. Help us joyfully to participate in your plan for our lives. We pray this through Jesus, our Saviour. Amen.*

Thought for the Day: I can trust the Potter to shape the best me.

Darlene Mackey (California)

PRAYER FOCUS: POTTERS

Working for God

Read 2 Thessalonians 3:6-13
Whatever you do, work at it with all your heart, as though you were working for the Lord and not for people. Colossians 3:23 (GNB)

After working with a title of 'minister' for many years, I now work outside the church as a mental-health counsellor. Even so, I don't feel any less a minister; my approach to this job is that of a Christian serving the Lord. Each person I see is a child of God. When I work with that in mind, my job becomes my ministry. Whatever job we have, whether it is a church job or a job in a secular field, we have opportunities to share the love of God.

I now see many people who would never enter a church, extending the reach of my ministry. One day a colleague asked me how I could treat our clients, who at times are belligerent, with such patience and kindness. I answered, 'Because I'm doing it for God.'

Each of us can look for opportunities to work for God in the way we do our daily tasks.

Prayer: *God of opportunities, open our eyes to those around us who may need to experience your love. Make our behaviour a witness of your love and grace. In Jesus' name we pray. Amen.*

Thought for the Day: Each of us can make our day's tasks a ministry.

Malinda Fillingim (Georgia)

Limps and Scars

Read Genesis 32:9-32

Forgetting what lies behind and straining forward to what lies ahead, I press on toward the goal for the prize of the heavenly call of God in Christ Jesus. Philippians 3:13-14 (NRSV)

One of my favourite Bible stories recounts Jacob wrestling with God. I like it because it reminds me of life's dark moments when my dreams crumble around me and I am down in the dirt, wrestling with God. At times like these I have asked myself, What good can possibly come from this? Jacob's story answers that question. Jacob came away from his battle with a new name, Israel, because he had struggled with God and with humans and had overcome (see Gen. 32:28). When we wrestle with God, we too become strengthened to overcome the trials ahead.

Like Jacob, we may come away with a limp or a scar. But often our scars can remind us to reach out to those who need the good news of hope in the midst of their own struggles.

The 'sun rose upon [Jacob]' (Gen. 32:31) as he moved on to deal with old struggles in a new way. Whatever our struggles may be, God helps us to leave yesterday's trials behind and to press on in hope towards tomorrow.

Prayer: *O Lord, in the battles of our lives, help us to find hope in you and your goodness. Amen.*

Thought for the Day: Wrestling with God opens the door to deeper relationship.

Dyton L. Owen (Oklahoma)

PRAYER FOCUS: THOSE FACING OVERWHELMING STRUGGLES

Surrendering All

Read Romans 10:1-13

Everyone who calls on the name of the Lord will be saved.
Romans 10:13 (NIV)

My mother was a British war veteran, the matriarch of our family, and an intelligent woman. But Mum did not know Jesus as her personal Saviour. She believed in God, but she had trouble with the concept of Jesus being divine. 'I believe Jesus was a great prophet,' she would say, 'but the Son of God?'

After Mum's stroke, she fought her way through many physical challenges. My heart broke as I watched my mother deteriorate before my eyes. Later she came to live with me. I had promised her many years earlier that I would care for her and not put her in an institution. For years I had been praying for my mother's salvation.

Three days before Mum died, God performed a miracle. Mum surrendered her life to the Lord — not because of anything I did or said. She looked heavenward and asked Jesus to be her Saviour. Perfect peace prevailed over Mum's remaining hours on this earth. She could hardly wait to be with Jesus.

God offers each of us salvation and eternal life. The choice is ours.

Prayer: *Father, you have declared in your word that salvation is available to all. Help us never to give up praying for those who do not know you. In Jesus' name we pray. Amen.*

Thought for the Day: Surrendering to Christ gives us ultimate freedom.

Glynis M. Belec (Ontario, Canada)

God Our Guide

Read Psalm 32

The LORD says, 'I will instruct thee and teach thee in the way which thou shalt go: I will guide thee with mine eye.' Psalm 32:8 (KJV)

With my fair skin and blonde hair, I could not hide the fact that I was a foreigner in northern China. My fair-haired travelling companion stood out even more because she was also tall. We tried to fit in, learning some Mandarin phrases and observing local customs. Still, everything was unfamiliar; we were aware that we were not at home.

One afternoon, we browsed in a crowded street market in Beijing. Suddenly, I felt panicky because I had lost sight of my friend. I was alone, thousands of miles from home. I stood on a corner slowly scanning the area, but I could not find her.

Then a woman caught my attention and pointed to where my friend had crouched down to study something in the market. With relief and gratitude, I beamed at the stranger and nodded my thanks.

Her kindness reminded me that God knows my every move as I travel in this foreign world, far from my eternal home. God knows what I need before I do. God knows the lie of the land and waits for me to look for direction.

Prayer: *Teach us, O God, to fix our eyes on you for guidance. Amen.*

Thought for the Day: Our all-seeing God is a trustworthy guide.

Dolly Dickinson (North Carolina)

Fleeting or Eternal?

Read 1 John 2:15-17

The world and its desire are passing away, but those who do the will of God live forever. 1 John 2:17 (NRSV)

One day in the early hours of the morning, I began to think about these words from John's epistle. What did John mean by them? Reflecting on this question, I realised that God wants us to focus attention on everlasting values. In today's text, the world's passing values are contrasted with God's eternal values. This world, with its variety of desires, is destined to perish, but those who do the will of God live forever.

How are things with me today? Am I eagerly looking to do God's will, following the example of Christ, who said, 'I seek to do not my own will but the will of him who sent me' (John 5:30, NRSV)? Am I living according to God's will? This is a key question for the Christian life.

Only Christ can save us from this world that is corrupted by sin and give us a new life here, as well as eternal life to come. The Holy Spirit provides us with the power to understand and to live according to God's will. As Paul wrote, 'Do not be conformed to this world, but be transformed by the renewing of your minds, so that you may discern what is the will of God — what is good and acceptable and perfect' (Rom. 12:2, NRSV).

Prayer: *O God, teach us to seek your will in everything. Help us to give up what is passing and unworthy in your sight. Amen.*

Thought for the Day: Seeking to do the will of God is the lifestyle of believers.

Toomas Pajusoo (Harjumaa, Estonia)

New Opportunities from God

Read Psalm 107:1-9

O give thanks to the LORD, for he is good; for his steadfast love endures forever. Psalm 107:1 (NRSV)

The Sandia Mountains in New Mexico display a constantly changing face as the weather and the location of the sun change. On some days the mountains appear dark and foreboding; on others, they glisten and shine as diamonds reflecting the rays of the sun. The most glorious change occurs when the sun is setting and the colours change from grey-green to vibrant pink or red.

Like the changing beauty of the mountains, God's presence and love appear in many different forms as well. When my wife and I lost our former spouses, life appeared dark and gloomy and reflected our sadness and sorrow. We were only in our 40s and never imagined that we would experience such loss at such an early age. We likewise had not thought we would face a struggle to understand how a loving God could leave us with so much pain. But new joy arrived when my wife and I met months later and discovered that God had prepared another chapter in our lives.

Some of life's changes we welcome, and others break our heart. In the midst of all of them, God sustains us, strengthens us, and brings us new hope with opportunities we could never have anticipated.

Prayer: *God of grace and mercy, open our hearts to your presence in the midst of all the changes and opportunities that come our way. Amen.*

Thought for the Day: Our God of love never leaves us in despair.

D. Max Whitfield (New Mexico)

PRAYER FOCUS: THOSE BEING MARRIED AGAIN

God is Able

Read Acts 12:1-19
Is any thing too hard for the LORD? Genesis 18:14 (KJV)

This morning I was reading Acts 12:1-19, the passage about Peter's imprisonment and his rescue by an angel of the Lord. As I read, God drew my attention to two details: the believers' prayer for Peter and their reaction to God's response to their prayers.

We read in verse 5 that the church was praying constantly for Peter. We aren't told the content of their prayers, but the believers no doubt asked God to deliver Peter. When Peter came to their door and Rhoda informed the believers, their response was disbelief. When Rhoda insisted that Peter was alive and outside the door, his friends thought that Peter's angel was visiting them. When they finally saw Peter for themselves, they were amazed.

Some elements of this passage are almost comical: the maid forgetting to open the door, Peter waiting stranded on the doorstep. The passage also reveals something about human nature. Jesus tells us, 'Whatsoever ye shall ask in prayer, believing, ye shall receive' (Matt. 21:22, KJV). How many times do we pray for something without believing that God is capable of doing what we ask? But the Bible tells us, 'With God, all things are possible' (Mk. 10:27, KJV).

Prayer: *God, strengthen our faith that we pray with confidence, and open our eyes to see how you answer. In Jesus' name. Amen.*

Thought for the Day: Sometimes the answer to our prayers is right in front of us.

Janine A. Kuty (Virginia)

Learning to Walk

Read Matthew 18:1-4

The God of compassion said, 'It was I who taught Ephraim to walk, I took them up in my arms.' Hosea 11:3 (NRSV)

I can remember the special days when our children took their first steps, their tiny hands holding my fingers for balance. In front of them was a new and wonderful world, one they could not see when they were crawling around on their own. They could not see me behind them, but they did not let go because they instinctively knew they would lose their balance without me. When they became strong and balanced enough to support themselves, I turned them around towards me. Once they could see me, the desire to come to me gave them the courage to take those first steps on their own into my arms. They stumbled a few times, but I was always there to catch them, strengthening their skill and faith in themselves so they could someday walk on their own.

As I read Jesus' words in Matthew 18, 'Unless you change and become like children' (v. 3, NRSV), I realise that I've been crawling along through life for too long on my own. When I allow God to guide me, I see a new world, an outlook I've never experienced before. Then as I turn to God in worship, prayer and service, I find confidence to take those first steps to God so that soon we can walk side by side.

Prayer: *God, help us to reach out to you, to trust you as our guide, and to look for your wondrous hand at work in your world. Amen.*

Thought for the Day: Amid the imbalances of life, reach out for the steadying hand of God.

Mark H. Anderson (Pennsylvania)

PRAYER FOCUS: FOR COURAGE TO TAKE A FIRST STEP

Bearing Fruit

Read John 15:1-8
Jesus said, 'I am the vine, you are the branches. Those who abide in me and I in them bear much fruit, because apart from me you can do nothing.' John 15:5 (NRSV)

As a young woman, I attended a week-long Christian conference. I struggled to go to the various meetings and lectures. Everyone seemed excited and talked about what they had learned — except me.

'Why, Lord, can't I join in?' I prayed. I knew the answer: I was just too depressed to be with others.

Walking around the beautiful grounds, I came across a majestic tree. A main branch had been torn off, probably in a storm. In its place was a great red gash, and sticky resin oozed out of the wound. Yet in spite of this damage, the tree was full of leaves and cones. The gash in this tree reminded me that I too had lost something in my life when my dad died.

Then I thought of the scripture passage which tells us that if we remain in Jesus, we will bear much fruit. Through his love and through caring people, Jesus Christ can heal the wounds in our lives.

Looking at the bountiful fruit on the tree that day, I saw that a damaged tree can bear much fruit. Like that tree, we can bear fruit in our lives even though we suffer.

Prayer: *Dear Lord, source of life and strength, help us to rely on you to heal our wounds. Amen.*

Thought for the Day: God uses damaged people.

Lynn Sara How (Cheshire, England)

Trusting God

Read Romans 8:37-39

Jesus answered [the thief], 'I tell you the truth, today you will be with me in paradise.' Luke 23:43 (NIV)

I belong to a Bible study group of older men. Each week we read and discuss scripture passages and meditations from *The Upper Room* using the guide in the back of the magazine.

In a recent meeting, one man asked, 'What is heaven?' The consensus was that while we have no specific, detailed description of heaven, we believe it is a wonderful place. Recalling this conversation, I remembered an experience from my youth.

One summer when I was about five, my family went to a lake on holiday. I put on my bathing suit and ran out to the end of the jetty, where I stopped and stood, looking down at the water. I hadn't yet learned to swim. Suddenly, I saw my Dad looking up at me from the water.

'Come on!' he called, holding his arms up. 'Jump to me!' I hesitated. 'I'll catch you; I promise.' He smiled up at me. 'It'll be all right. Trust me.'

Mustering my courage, I jumped and dropped into his arms. 'See?' he said, 'I said it would be okay.'

Though we do not know what heaven will be like, we can trust that God meets us there. As my father caught me when I jumped fearfully off the jetty, our heavenly Father is always there for us.

Prayer: *God, give us faith to rely on your love. Amen.*

Thought for the Day: God waits to embrace us, here and on the other side of death.

Tuck Eudy (Florida)

PRAYER FOCUS: MEN'S GROUPS

It is God's

Read Deuteronomy 8:11-20

Do not say to yourself, 'My power and the might of my own hand have gained me this wealth.' Deuteronomy 8:17 (NRSV)

At dinner, my husband and I joined two people we didn't know. When their meal came, they bowed their heads and said a prayer. I smiled. 'Seeing someone else pray before a meal is so nice.'

The young woman responded, 'Well, why not? The food we eat comes from God.' I appreciated her simple, matter-of-fact answer.

We work day after day so that we have money to buy what we need to survive and to give us pleasure. We could easily say, 'I worked for this. I earned it. It's mine.'

The truth is, God created the earth and everything on it. God created us and gave us intricate minds and bodies. God gives us strength, initiative, intelligence and the good sense to use them.

Yes, we work to earn money for food, but God gives us the ability to work to earn a living. God also causes the seeds to grow so food is available. God is indeed the source of all good things.

Prayer: *God, remind us that you are the source of our strength, power and will. Amen.*

Thought for the Day: God is the source of all that is good.

Margie J. Harding (Maryland)

Time Enough

Read Matthew 6:25-34

Do not worry about tomorrow, for tomorrow will bring worries of its own. Today's trouble is enough for today. Matthew 6:34 (NRSV)

Modern technology allows us to both speed up and slow down time. In a television-makeover programme, a garden or home is transformed in minutes. But in real life beautiful gardens take years of hard work, and redecorating is not as easy as it looks on TV. On the other hand, modern technology can also slow down time, as we see in the endless slow-motion replays of decisive moments in sporting events. The past is gone; the future comes at its own pace. In reality, we cannot rewind or speed up our life.

We may be tempted to look back with regret, anger and resentment at all our dashed hopes, at all our 'if onlys'. Or at times we may consider the future bleak and want to rush past it. But we cannot alter time. What we have is God's gift of today and the freedom to choose how to live it.

The Apostle Paul gave us an example of how to put the past behind us when he wrote, 'Forgetting what is behind... I press on toward the goal to win the prize for which God has called me heavenward in Christ Jesus' (Phil. 3:13-14, NIV). Like Paul, we can take each day's opportunity to use the gifts that God has given us.

Prayer: *O God, may we choose to use our time wisely, always grateful for all your gifts. Amen.*

Thought for the Day: Worrying about the past or the future keeps us from taking joy in the present.

Anne Rasmussen (Somerset, England)

Times of Refreshing

Read Psalm 51:1-12

Repent… and turn to God, so that your sins may be wiped out, that times of refreshing may come from the Lord. Acts 3:19 (NIV)

As a teenager, I helped my father harvest hay each autumn. It was a hot and dirty job. We picked up the bales from the field and stacked them on a wagon. Inevitably, hay would rain down on me as I placed the bales on the wagon. The dusty debris would find its way into my clothing, my hair and often my eyes. It would irritate my hot, sweaty skin. Oh, how I would long for a refreshing shower to wash the dirt and debris from my body!

Sin makes our soul just as dirty — and also breaks our relationship with a holy God (see Isa. 59:2). Today's reading is a prayer of repentance. King David prayed this prayer after being confronted by Nathan the prophet about his adultery with Bathsheba and the murder of Uriah. David recognised that his sins had separated him from God. As the psalm tells us, David understood that sincere repentance restores our relationship with God, and brings 'times of refreshing'.

At times we all have spiritual dirt in our lives. But when we examine ourselves and seek God's forgiveness, we too can experience 'times of refreshing'.

Prayer: *Wash away our sins, dear God, and restore to us 'the joy of your salvation' (see Ps. 51:12). Amen.*

Thought for the Day: When we repent, forgiveness washes over us.

Terry Thomas Bowman (North Carolina)

A Lawn to Mow

Read Luke 10:25-37
The teacher of the Law wanted to justify himself, so he asked Jesus, 'Who is my neighbour?' Luke 10:29 (GNB)

'Hey, can you come over here?' yelled Ruby, leaning against her doorway. I walked across the garden to her. She asked if I knew someone who could mow her lawn. I explained that I was visiting my daughter and didn't know anyone in town. I offered a sheepish smile and told her I would let her know if I heard of anyone who cuts grass. She took a deep breath from her oxygen canister and thanked me.

Of course, I was perfectly capable of mowing her lawn, but I justified myself by making excuses for not helping Ruby: I take care of my 81-year-old mother; I help my children and grandchildren; I work at my church; Ruby is not my responsibility. But even to me, my excuses sounded lame. In Matthew 19:19 Jesus says, 'Love your neighbour as yourself' (NRSV). Ruby needed to see God's love in my love for her.

Pushing the mower to Ruby's small patch of lawn, I cranked the machine to life. Cutting the grass helped Ruby, and my action pleased God.

I realised then that our days are filled with chances to help our neighbours. Practising kindness and easing someone's burden says we are trying to live a life of love — the life God wants us to live.

Prayer: *Remind me, Lord, to help my neighbours, rich or poor, young or old, no matter where they live. Help me to show Jesus to all people. Amen.*

Thought for the Day: When I see a need I can meet, God wants me to meet it.

Irene Pruett-Wilson (Texas)

God's Daily Mercy

Read Isaiah 43:1-4

The steadfast love of the LORD never ceases, his mercies never come to an end; they are new every morning. Lamentations 3:22-23 (NRSV)

My sister, who is in the hospital, endures terrible pain from serious kidney disease. I know and understand that God does not rejoice in her suffering. Rather, God knows our condition and offers us divine mercy. This mercy washes over our anguish with the balm of pure, divine love.

We don't understand why there is so much suffering in the world. Indeed, something inside us seeks a reason for our adversity. Then, in our struggle to understand, we realise that God offers us something more: love and mercy that sustain us when we are weak. Each time we cry out, 'Lord, save me', God reaches out to wrap loving arms around us, again and again. Suffering can teach us to understand the value of life and the power of God's love.

Prayer: *Gracious Lord, thank you for being the beacon of mercy and love that shines through our grief, and for sustaining us in our time of need. As Jesus taught us, we pray, 'Our Father which art in heaven, Hallowed be thy name. Thy kingdom come. Thy will be done in earth, as it is in heaven. Give us this day our daily bread. And forgive us our debts, as we forgive our debtors. And lead us not into temptation, but deliver us from evil: For thine is the kingdom, and the power, and the glory, for ever. Amen.'**

Thought for the Day: God's mercy sustains us in any adversity.

Jesús Quintanilla Osorio (Quintana Roo, Mexico)

*Matthew 6:9-13 (KJV)

Maybe Tomorrow

Read 1 Thessalonians 1:1-10

There is still a vision for the appointed time; it speaks of the end, and does not lie. If it seems to tarry, wait for it; it will surely come, it will not delay.
Habakkuk 2:3 (NRSV)

After my first term in a theological college in the USA, I returned to my homeland, Ukraine, for a visit. When it was time to leave, I told my family that I would return again soon. Each of us had a different understanding of 'soon' — in six months, in a year, after graduation. But no one really thought that my second return would take so long. Six years have passed; many events have taken place in our lives since. But I have not been home again yet.

When my parents heard that I had finally received permanent-resident status in the USA, they expected me to come home at any moment. In preparation for my expected arrival, they make sure they have a good provision of everything. Every time they hear a car passing by their house, they hope it is me arriving. But it is not. 'Maybe tomorrow,' they say.

In Acts 1:11 we read about Jesus leaving his disciples. They believed he would be back soon. In 1 Thessalonians Paul praises the believers in Thessalonica for their deeds of love while waiting for Christ's second coming. Now we are waiting. As we wait, we serve Christ in those around us, while saying, 'Come, Lord Jesus, come!'

Prayer: *God of hope, give us perseverance and courage to take advantage of our opportunities as we wait for your second coming. In Jesus' name we pray. Amen.*

Thought for the Day: Our hope as believers in Christ will end in gladness.

Yulia G. Bagwell (Pennsylvania)

PRAYER FOCUS: FAMILIES WAITING FOR A LOVED ONE

The Lord's Presence

Read Hebrews 10:19-25
Where two or three come together in my name, there am I with them.
Matthew 18:20 (NIV)

One morning I went to my friend's house. I knocked on the door; and when my friend opened the door, he was holding his Bible and The Upper Room daily devotional guide. I realised that this was the time for his morning prayers.

I joined him. My friend read from the Bible, his wife read The Upper Room meditation and I was given the opportunity to pray. The 'Prayer Focus' was for those who suffered from paralysis. We named two people, and I prayed for them.

After prayer, my friend invited me to join them every morning for fellowship with a Bible reading, the meditation from The Upper Room and prayer. I experienced the Lord's presence in this small breakfast fellowship. I saw great joy on the faces of my friend and his wife. This unexpected morning fellowship has inspired me in my life with Christ.

Prayer: *Heavenly Lord, bless us each time we open the Bible and pray. In Jesus' name. Amen.*

Thought for the Day: When have I found unexpected fellowship with God's people?

Yakub L. Mekwan (Gujarat, India)

Food for Thought

Read Psalm 103:1-14

He has told you, O mortal, what is good; and what does the LORD require of you but to do justice, and to love kindness, and to walk humbly with your God? Micah 6:8 (NRSV)

This is my 94th year, and I spend a great deal of time reminiscing about the different stages of my life. I especially like to think about my happy childhood. I had loving parents who tried to teach Christian values and habits both by word and example. These values influenced my life through my teenage years and adulthood, and now they influence me in this stage of my life.

As I looked through a scrapbook of materials I've collected over the years, the following question gave me food for thought: When I die, will the world be a better place because I have lived or because I have died?

If I am to evaluate my life honestly, I also must ask other questions: Have I loved my neighbour as myself? Have I treated others as I want them to treat me? Have I done what Micah says God requires of me: 'To do justice, and to love kindness, and to walk humbly with [my] God'?

I know I have failed many times in many ways. But how thankful I am that God is merciful and forgiving and that I can say, 'Lord, I am trying.'

Prayer: *Thank you, compassionate God, for life. Thank you for your love and for your forgiveness when we fail to do your will. Amen.*

Thought for the Day: It's never too late to help God change the world.

Billie E. Kemp (Tennessee)

PRAYER FOCUS: THOSE NEARING THEIR 100th BIRTHDAY

God's Blessing

Read Zephaniah 3:14-20
Turn, O LORD, and deliver me; save me because of your unfailing love.
Psalm 6:4 (NIV)

For many years I was able to tell people that God had blessed me with good health. Then in 2005 I was diagnosed with cancer. For someone who had experienced only minor illnesses in his life, cancer was quite a shock.

All through my cancer treatment, many of my friends prayed for me. I experienced some anxious moments, but I was always aware that those who loved me were praying for me and asking God to support me. I began to realise that I still had the greatest blessing of all — God's unconditional love, shown through the support of loved ones and friends.

I am doing very well now and have won my battle with cancer. But if things had not gone well, or if the cancer returns in the future, I still have the blessing of God's love for me, no matter what.

Now I simply tell people that God has blessed me with love that is greater than any struggle I may face.

Prayer: *Dear God, thank you for your love that never leaves us. Help us to remember that you are always with us even through our darkest times. Amen.*

Thought for the Day: God's power is greater than any problem we face.

Glen Graham (Louisiana)

Unlimited Love

Read Ephesians 3:14-21
Neither height nor depth, nor anything else in all creation, will be able to separate us from the love of God that is in Christ Jesus Our Lord.
Romans 8:39 (NIV)

Our daughter and son-in-law and three young granddaughters live far from home. They are on a different continent, across the Atlantic Ocean, in another hemisphere and in a different time zone. Whenever we visit, we enjoy every moment of our fellowship. Just after a recent visit, I thought about my daughter — how much I love her and how much I would miss her. And I knew that even though we are separated physically by oceans and continents, nothing can stop the love we share.

Wherever our loved ones may live in the world, we will always be linked together by love. This can show us something about how I hear this truth. The words of an old gospel song are simple yet true: 'Wide, wide, as the ocean, high as the heaven above; deep, deep as the deepest sea is my Saviour's love.'

God's love reaches all of us, wherever we are.

Prayer: *Thank you, God, that nobody is beyond the reach of your love. Bless those far from home and family, and keep us all in your care. Amen.*

Thought for the Day: Love links us to God and to each other.

Penny Wellington (Gauteng, South Africa)

Our Ninevites

Read Jonah 3:4 – 4:11

Love your enemies and pray for those who persecute you, so that you may be children of your Father in heaven. Matthew 5:44-45 (NRSV)

Jonah was furious that God forgave Israel's enemies, the Ninevites, when they repented. His bitterness kept him in the blistering sun for 40 days as he watched the city, hoping God would exchange mercy for wrath. I used to be perplexed that Jonah could resent the Ninevites that much. Then I thought back to a time, when I worked in a construction crew under a seasoned foreman I will call 'Jack'. On the job, Jack constantly yelled at the rest of us, using foul language to insult our intelligence and skills. When we were away from home Jack would sometimes come in from a night of drinking and snack on the food we had bought for our lunches.

One night I read Matthew 5:44-45 and decided to pray for my enemy, Jack. I asked God to save him, but my heart wasn't really in my prayer. Years after had I left that job, I met a man from Jack's hometown and asked about Jack, hoping for bad news. The man informed me that Jack was a pastor in that town. I was shocked and, deep down, a little disappointed. Where's the justice in that? I thought. Like Jonah, I knew that we serve a God of compassion, and I had feared that my half-hearted prayer would be answered. I've since thanked God for showing compassion to Jack because it's the same compassion God has granted to me.

Prayer: *Forgiving God, be with those who wish us harm. Help us to pray for them and to reveal your glory to them through our love. Amen.*

Thought for the Day: God's love can transform our enemies — and us.

Brian Slate (Kansas)

Fungus among Us

Read Psalm 139:7-12

If I go up to the heavens, you are there; if I make my bed in the depths, you are there. Psalm 139:8 (NIV)

While tourists on holiday, my husband and I walked down into a coal mine. We went only 300 feet into the mine's depths, but we still experienced the intense feeling of being completely isolated in the cold, damp underground. The tour guide put off the lights so that we could experience the oppressive force of total darkness.

While we were still deep within the mine, he turned his helmet light back on. When he did, I noticed something sticking out of a wooden support beam in the passageway ceiling. A closer inspection revealed three white pieces of fungus — life, even here!

On reflection, I realised that even in the depths of the earth, God is present. What a comforting thought! No matter where we are, whether over, on or under this earth, we are never alone. God is always with us.

Prayer: *Thank you, dear Lord, for showing us signs of your presence; for assuring us that you are always with us; and for giving us faith that whatever our circumstances, we can abide in your love. Amen.*

Thought for the Day: In life's darkest moments, God offers us life.

Sue Gordon (Ontario, Canada)

PRAYER FOCUS: MINERS AND THEIR FAMILIES

The Most Important Thing

Read John 10:22-30
Jesus said, 'My sheep listen to my voice; I know them, and they follow me.'
John 10:27 (NIV)

'What is most important?' That was the question going through my mind on my day off. The answer was suddenly obvious: 'The most important thing is to visit Mary!' I'd been meaning to visit Mary, a member of my church who had returned home from the hospital a few weeks earlier, but I hadn't got round to it. I changed course and headed for Mary's house.

That afternoon, Mary told me of her love of reading, and she asked me to read to her on my next visit. I volunteered to read in the remaining time I had that afternoon. The book I read captivated us both, so I continued reading past the time I should have. I promised to visit every Friday afternoon to read to her and eagerly looked forward to my next visit.

Two days later, I was devastated to learn that Mary had died the day after my visit. There would be no more stories of Mary's childhood, no more afternoons of reading together. But I am grateful to God for that afternoon. How many times have I known what is right and not acted upon it? Because I responded to God, my day took an unexpected turn — one that has helped me to remember what is most important: listening to God.

Prayer: *Dear God, help us to hear your voice and to respond. Amen.*

Thought for the Day: If we ask and listen, God will lead us to what is most important for us.

Laurie Juliana (Virginia)

Writing Prayers

Read Luke 17:11-19

We give thanks to you, O God, we give thanks to you! We proclaim how great you are and tell of the wonderful things you have done.
Psalm 75:1 (GNB)

I keep a book of prayers that I've written. The book is nothing fancy — a small spiral notebook, rather frayed. I write in it prayer requests and thanks to God. I began doing this about 10 years ago when I read a book on prayer. The author suggested recording prayers as a method of increasing our focus and intent. I write prayers on matters that concern and worry me, and I write a list of special blessings and pleasant surprises for which I am thankful.

If I'm honest, I have to admit that my requests far outnumber my prayers of thanksgiving. I tend to list my petitions more than I recount God's wondrous deeds. I personify the 10 lepers all by myself (Luke 17), giving thanks perhaps once for every nine times I take God's blessings for granted.

Now as I read back over my prayers that expressed fear and worry, I realise that God has addressed each one. Sometimes my prayers were answered as I had hoped. At other times, God blessed me with an unexpected answer. Some of my prayers are still unanswered. For each prayer I've written, God has touched me with love, mercy and compassion.

Prayer: *Dear God, teach us to live in ways that express thanksgiving and praise. Amen.*

Thought for the Day: When you pray, prepare to be surprised.

Bruce Bedingfield (Illinois)

PRAYER FOCUS: TO BE MORE AWARE OF GOD'S BLESSINGS

A 'Sign' of Faith

Read Hebrews 11:6, 32-40
Faith is… what the ancients were commended for. Hebrews 11:1-2 (NIV)

When I was in college many years ago, a friend of mine made a small wooden sign for my dormitory door. It was stained dark brown with white letters that read, 'Have Faith in God'. Those words were both a challenge and a hope to me then, and they have remained so to this day.

They challenge me because — despite countless trips past that sign — I have not always adhered to its timeless admonition. Sometimes when job uncertainties or family losses have arisen, I have been slow to trust God. Even happy times have sometimes subtly robbed me of the vigilance I need to cultivate my faith.

But these words inspire hope as well. Hebrews 11 reminds me that by faith some of the Bible's most humble characters rose above their circumstances and their failings to please our Creator. Reading about them I gain new hope and encouragement.

Prayer: *Lord Jesus, thank you for the commendable lives of your faithful people. In every circumstance may we also have faith in God. Amen.*

Thought for the Day: God rejoices in our growing faith.

Steve Wilcox (Kentucky)

Blessed by Beauty

Read Psalm 104:1-24

The earth is the LORD'S, and the fulness thereof. Psalm 24:1 (KJV)

I live in the beautiful city of Cape Town in South Africa. On my way home from dropping my children at school, I often go into a botanical garden situated on the slopes of Table Mountain. I spend half an hour walking, communing with God, before I start my day's work.

As I walk, I feel exhilarated by the fresh air, the sun on my face and the rhythm of my body as I move. I am immersed in a feast for the senses: the glint of sunlight on water, the flash of red as a bird darts across my path, the rich scent of plants, and the calls of birds that fill the air. Towering against the brilliant blue of the sky is Table Mountain with its white tablecloth of cloud.

I walk nearly every day. If it's raining, I enjoy feeling the rain on my face, knowing that in our dry climate, water is life. I always return home feeling refreshed. My body is energised by the walk, my spirits are lifted, my hope is revived, and my heart rejoices in the beauty of the world God has given us. I am thankful for those who work to maintain this beautiful place and for the way God feeds my spirit through it. I am thankful for this and for all the ways God speaks to me.

Prayer: *God, thank you for your gift of Earth, our beautiful home. Help us to honour your gift by taking care of it, preserving its beauty, managing its resources wisely and taking time to enjoy it. Amen.*

Thought for the Day: Appreciating the world God has given us is an act of worship.

Sally Argent (Cape Town, South Africa)

PRAYER FOCUS: THAT THOSE IN POWER SAFEGUARD THE EARTH

A Promise

Read John 14:1-4

Jesus said, 'And if I go and prepare a place for you, I will come back and take you to be with me that you also may be where I am.'
John 14:3 (NIV)

Years ago, we watched our five-year-old son lose his fight for life. That loss still leaves a permanent void in my life. I faced a double portion of grief as I thought of telling our six-year-old daughter that her brother had died and was now in heaven. We chose to tell her in a beautiful spot on a hilltop in a secluded rural area. She seemed pleased with the knowledge that Danny was no longer ill but in heaven. She looked up at the sky and asked, 'Is he in the blue part or the white part?'

Much time has passed, but I often reflect on my conversation with my daughter that day. Jesus spoke of God's providing room in heaven for all who believe.

Assurance of our final home is found in Jesus' words: 'I am going there to prepare a place for you' (John 14:2, NIV). Now I understand that Jesus may not have been speaking of a place at all but of something more meaningful: a promise that where he is, we will be also.

Prayer: *Dear God, help us to trust Christ's promise of an eternity where we are held within your love. Amen.*

Thought for the Day: The place God has prepared for us will be better than whatever we can imagine.

Don Wallace (Arkansas)

Makers of Peace

Read James 3:13-18
Blessed are the peacemakers, for they will be called children of God.
Matthew 5:9 (NRSV)

I remember when I first realised that Jesus and James did not speak of blessings coming to those who keep the peace but rather to those who make peace. There is a difference. Some seek to keep the peace by brushing conflict under the carpet — by not dealing with issues that ought to concern us or by keeping quiet when someone needs us to speak out. Others make peace by being reconcilers, by building unity between individuals and groups, by helping persons appreciate the viewpoint of others and love them — in spite of differences and in the midst of conflict.

At times I have tried to keep the peace by withdrawing or even by avoiding people with whom I might disagree. This could be called peacekeeping, but it is not the active love that Jesus and James spoke of as peacemaking. True peacemaking is an act of love that works for reconciliation and for the good of each person. Jesus blessed peacemakers, calling them children of God. We live out our identity as God's children when we become true peacemakers, when we take on Christ's nature of love, forgiveness and reconciliation.

Prayer: *O God, help us not only to keep the peace but to work to make peace in all our relationships. Amen.*

Thought for the Day: We follow Christ when we reconcile and make peace.

John M. Drescher (Pennsylvania)

PRAYER FOCUS: THOSE WORKING FOR PEACE

A Priceless Treasure

Read Romans 12:9-16
This is the day the LORD has made; let us rejoice and be glad in it.
Psalm 118:24 (NIV)

I met Marian at a writing conference. We had both wanted a roommate, and those in charge of the conference put us together. A friendship developed, and we have stayed in touch for 20 years. Marian and I have offered each other a shoulder to cry on and talked about our happiness, hopes, and dreams.

For birthdays, we select special gifts for each other. One year for my birthday, Marian gave me a bracelet with a charm shaped like a box. I have worn it for many years. Recently, on one of those days when everything was going wrong, I noticed the box on the bracelet, and it dawned on me that maybe it opened. I discovered that it did. Inside was a rolled-up piece of paper. With a pair of tweezers, I took the paper out, and, with much anticipation, opened it. I read, 'This is the day the Lord has made; let us rejoice and be glad in it' (Ps. 118:24, NIV).

That message had been hidden away for 10 years, but it came to light at a time when I needed to hear its words. They reminded me that each new day is a gift and a reason for rejoicing. Putting a smile on my face, I thanked God for the day and for Marian, who conveyed a message of joy.

Prayer: *Thank you, God, for the gift of each new day and for friends who remind us of your grace. Amen.*

Thought for the Day:
Every day look for reasons to rejoice.

Pat Stackhouse (Indiana)

The Master Player

Read Galatians 2:19-21

I have been crucified with Christ and I no longer live, but Christ lives in me. The life I live in the body, I live by faith in the Son of God, who loved me and gave himself for me. Galatians 2:20 (NIV)

I watched as my sister carefully strummed the strings of the guitar. After several attempts to explain to her the technique and to demonstrate it, I realised that another approach was required. Stepping behind her, I put my hand over hers. 'Let me control the stroke, and then you'll be able to feel how this is supposed to work.'

My sister consented, but as I started to move her arm, I could feel her resisting. 'Just let me control the stroke,' I repeated. But, again, I could feel her trying to move the pick across the strings.

Later, as I pondered this, Galatians 2:20 came to mind. My sister was not able to allow me to guide her hands. I found myself asking how often I agree to allow the Spirit to control my life only to immediately attempt to perform 'righteous' acts from my own strength and understanding instead. I realise now that only by permitting the Spirit to work through me will I ever be able to truly follow Christ.

Prayer: *Dear Father, forgive us for the times when we depend only on our own strength. Teach us to rely on your Spirit, trusting you to work what is good through us. Amen.*

Thought for the Day: Only by allowing God to guide us will we become master players.

Anna C. Gheen (Idaho)

PRAYER FOCUS: MUSICIANS

Save the Seeds

Read 2 Timothy 3:14–4:5

But as for you, continue in what you have learned and have become convinced of, because you know those from whom you have learned it, and how from infancy you have known the holy Scriptures, which are able to make you wise for salvation through faith in Christ Jesus.
2 Timothy 3:14-15 (NIV)

Due to my mother's ill-health, my brothers and sisters and I were responsible for clearing her vegetable garden after the harvest. As we cleared away the plants, she instructed us, 'Save the seeds!' An avid gardener, she knew the unique hope in each tiny seed.

In the spring after she died, we discovered the seeds. As she had taught us, we planted the garden. We worked together joyfully, placing each seed into the soil; and eventually we shared a bountiful harvest.

By the end of another growing season, I came to realise a deeper meaning in my mother's words. We are to 'save the seeds' of our faith and plant the good news of God's love. Our responsibility is to carry the word of God into the world so that others may be saved. We may not plant her garden again next spring, but each of us will continue to plant tiny seeds of faith. In tending her garden, I have found my own. Every day is a good day to plant seeds.

Prayer: *Thank you, God, for the gift of faith from those who exemplify the love of Christ. Give us the strength to continue to plant seeds of faith in the world. Amen.*

Thought for the Day: How am I sowing seeds of my faith?

Kathy Powell (North Carolina)

Free to Serve

Read 1 Peter 4:12-16

What does the LORD require of you? To act justly and to love mercy and to walk humbly with your God. Micah 6:8 (NIV)

Week after week, I look at people in my congregation at my church. Many are 'regulars', but some are new people. People come with Bibles in hand, joyously singing and praising God. After church we have tea and a chat. Then everyone leaves. Most I will see next Sunday. A few will be involved in various church activities such as small groups, but most will not see one another until next Sunday.

As I think of our religious freedom, I compare our situation to that of our brothers and sisters in other countries who are persecuted for being Christians. Can we imagine how lonely they must feel? People are still being imprisoned and victimised for loving our Lord and Saviour, for reading the Bible, for going to church.

We who are free to serve God openly can use our time more productively. We are free to use our resources to help others who don't know God and don't go to church. We can help those far away by praying and contributing to provide Bibles for them. What other ways can you think of to use the time and freedom God has given us?

Prayer: *Lord, please be with your flock worldwide, especially those Christians living in a minority. Amen.*

Thought for the Day: We who are free to serve God have an obligation to live our faith openly.

Shaun McHardy (Cape Town, South Africa)

The Walk

Read Philippians 4:4-9

Give liberally and be ungrudging when you do so, for on this account the LORD your God will bless you in all your work and in all that you undertake. Deuteronomy 15:10 (NRSV)

While my two preschool-age children played at the park with my husband, I went for a walk. We had recently discovered that I was pregnant. Though I rejoiced, I was also troubled. Every day was the same: I changed nappies, put away toys, read children's books and answered lots of questions. I wondered, 'What is the purpose of it all?'

I came to an open church and wandered in. I sat in the front row and prayed, 'Why am I doing this?'

As I prayed, I realised that I wasn't living my life in thanksgiving for God's many blessings, particularly for the sacrifice of Christ. I had allowed daily tasks to take away the joy of simply following Christ, and I had developed a grudging heart. After a time of prayer, I dried my eyes and was able to go back to the playground to join my family with a cheerful heart.

These days, I remember that no matter what God gives me to do in life, I can 'do it all in the name of the Lord Jesus, giving thanks to God the Father through him' (Col. 3:17, NIV).

Prayer: *Thank you, God, for all your blessings and for reminders of your gracious love. Amen.*

Thought for the Day: If we follow Christ, our daily tasks can become the work of God.

Sonya A. Haskins (Tennessee)

Hope Amid Destruction

Read Jeremiah 30:1-9

'The days are coming,' declares the LORD, 'when I will bring my people Israel and Judah back from captivity and restore them to the land I gave to their forefathers to possess,' says the LORD. Jeremiah 30:3 (NIV)

As a doctor, I had the privilege of being a part of a medical team that was sent to an area devastated by an earthquake. Many lives had been lost and buildings destroyed.

Our relief team talked to people who had survived, sharing the good news of Jesus Christ wherever opportunity arose. Gradually, I could see God at work. The victims of the earthquake were looking for purpose in life after losing much — even some of their loved ones. Because the disaster had opened doors for us to share God's love with the people in a practical way, bringing both physical and spiritual healing, the people began to turn to God.

Jeremiah prophesied the destruction of Jerusalem and exile to Babylon. For God's people, that was not good news. Yet Jeremiah also prophesied later that God would bring restoration. Jeremiah saw something positive in the midst of destruction — God renewing the covenant. And God still does that for us.

Prayer: *Lord, help us to see your presence and hope in every dark situation. Amen.*

Thought for the Day: God can use even tragic situations and circumstances for divine purposes.

Ajit Barkataki (Maharashtra, India)

PRAYER FOCUS: SURVIVORS OF NATURAL CALAMITIES

Interruptions or Opportunities?

Read Mark 10:46-52

Jesus said [to Bartimaeus], 'What do you want me to do for you?'
Mark 10:51 (NRSV)

A young social worker complained to her supervisor that she had difficulty completing her work. 'The trouble is,' she said, 'people keep interrupting me.' Her supervisor replied, 'But, those interruptions are your work.'

We all experience interruptions. However, we can also see possibilities that come to us with them. Looking back, most of us can see how some of the most important relationships we have made, some of the most rewarding services we have performed, have come from what we first saw as interruptions.

Jesus gives us a model for dealing with interruptions. During Jesus' final journey to Jerusalem, blind Bartimaeus boldly called out, 'Jesus, Son of David, have mercy on me!' (Mark 10:47, NRSV). This journey to Jerusalem was an important moment in Jesus' ministry; the salvation of the world was at stake! But Jesus heard Bartimaeus, stopped and healed him.

We can never justify disregarding God's children. The interruptions in our lives may be God calling us to serve.

Prayer: *Teach us, Lord Jesus, always to be sensitive to the cry of someone in need. Amen.*

Thought for the Day: The Christian's business is caring for people.

Bill Adams (Queensland, Australia)

God Makes it Easy

Read Malachi 3:8-12

Bring the full tithe into the storehouse, so that there may be food in my house, and thus put me to the test, says the LORD of hosts; see if I will not open the windows of heaven for you and pour down for you an overflowing blessing. Malachi 3:10 (NRSV)

For some people, tithing seems difficult. How can I give the first 10 per cent of what I earn to God when money is tight and there are bills to pay? Yet on closer examination, we find that God makes it easy for us to obey this simple request. Everything we have actually belongs to God; we are merely stewards of what God has given us.

Ten per cent is not much, really. A candidate running for office who receives only 10 per cent of the vote will lose. If professional baseball players get a hit only once out of 10, they probably won't be in the team for very long. What about business? If you had a partnership with someone and your partner got 90 per cent of the profits while you got only 10 per cent, that wouldn't seem fair. But consider that God is the senior partner in our life, yet asks for only the first 10 per cent.

God says 'test me in this' so that we can experience the love and blessing God wants for us.

Prayer: *Teach us, O God, how to give lovingly to you a tithe of all you give to us. Amen.*

Thought for the Day: The Bible's standard of giving starts at 10 per cent.

John D. Bown (Minnesota)

PRAYER FOCUS: THOSE STRUGGLING TO GIVE TO GOD

Hope for the Living

Read Mark 2:1-12

Anyone who is among the living has hope. Ecclesiastes 9:4 (NIV)

Over the past 20 years, I have watched my sister self-destruct through drug use. I have been furious about her manipulation, lies and denial. Her behaviour has been devastating. She is no longer accepted in my parents' home or, for the safety of my children, in mine. She had a child out of wedlock, and the child's father died of a drug overdose.

My sister has not been willing to get help. My family and I have not been hopeful that this once fun-loving, carefree person will change and live in healthier, wiser ways.

The death of my niece's father brought me to my knees. I cried out in anger and heartbreak for the child. God took my anger towards my sister and transformed my heart with love and forgiveness. God reminded me that as long as my sister lives, there is hope — though hope may seem to be the size of a grain of sand. My job is to continue to pray, to love her, and to use any opportunity to point her to God.

Prayer: *God, remind us that hope is always there for those who are rebellious. We pray as Jesus taught us, saying, as we pray, 'Father, hallowed be your name, your kingdom come. Give us each day our daily bread. Forgive us our sins, for we also forgive everyone who sins against us. And lead us not into temptation.'* Amen.*

Thought for the Day: Never stop praying for those you love.

Christine Thompson (Florida)

144 **PRAYER FOCUS:** THOSE DEALING WITH ADDICTED LOVED ONES
   **Luke 11:2-4 (NIV)

Joyful Testimony

Read John 4:4-39

Many of the Samaritans from that town believed in [Jesus] because of the woman's testimony, 'He told me everything I ever did.'
John 4:39 (NIV)

Sometimes I hesitate to talk about God with those around me. Feeling inadequate, I wonder how I can explain that Jesus is alive and loves us deeply. Arguing will not persuade them of the truth. Today's reading showed me how one woman successfully shared the good news about Jesus.

Quite simply, the woman at the well could not hide her excitement. 'Come, see a man who told me everything I ever did' (v. 29) she exclaimed, eager for others to get to know him, too. Instead of a clever argument, she enthusiastically described her meeting with the Saviour, making him real to those who listened.

So when I struggle to find the right words, I think of the Samaritan woman and remind myself that I can simply explain that God knows all about me — the good and the bad — and still loves and accepts me. Why would I make sharing the gospel more complicated than this? No amount of clever arguments will win hearts as much as will our communicating the joy of knowing God — and the joy of God's knowing all about us and loving us anyway.

Prayer: *God of all knowledge, so fill us with joy that talking about you is easy and natural. Amen.*

Thought for the Day: Witnessing means talking about what we know of God.

Emma J. Peterson (Buckinghamshire, England)

PRAYER FOCUS: FOR WILLINGNESS TO SPEAK OF MY FAITH

Answering God's Call

Read Colossians 1:3-14

We are God's workmanship, created in Christ Jesus to do good works, which God prepared in advance for us to do. Ephesians 2:10 (NIV)

When I was young, my dad had a zip-up cardigan sweater that I liked to wear. It was a little scratchy and way too big for me; but when I put it on, it was like being wrapped in his arms. Dad died a few years ago, and now the sweater is mine. It's much softer now; it also fits me better! Best of all, I still feel as if my dad's arms are wrapped around me when I wear it.

That sweater is a lot like my Christian walk. Along the way I have been asked to do things that didn't seem to be the 'right fit' but I did them anyway. Some were straightforward, simple tasks, such as learning to read the Bible. Others were more challenging, such as taking a mission trip or leading a new ministry at church. Each such task seemed daunting when I was first asked to do it.

But God uses us in the way God needs us. I find that the more I journey into the tasks God has for me, the more comfortable I become with trying on new roles in serving the Lord.

When God speaks to us about doing some good work, we can go ahead and put on that sweater. It may be the perfect fit. And even if it is not, we may grow into it over time.

Prayer: *Lord, help us to hear you calling us to bring your light into the world in the ways that you have chosen for us. Amen.*

Thought for the Day: To what work is God calling me today?

Trish Krider (Florida)

A Lost Sheep

Read Luke 15:1-7
The LORD says, 'I will come to you and save you.' Jeremiah 30:11 (GNB)

At one point in my life, my faith began to falter. I had abandoned my God and the strong faith I had had from childhood. I was no longer wearing my cross, the symbol that constantly reminded me of Jesus' sacrifice. I had even removed all religious pictures from my walls. I had had enough of religious dogma. I had not prayed for many days, and I felt lost. Eventually, when I could not bear my situation any longer, I turned to God for help.

I took the Bible from my bookshelf and held it in my hands, uttering desperately, 'If there is a God, please help me. Maybe there is something you would like to tell me, Lord.' Then I opened my Bible and read these words: 'I am the Lord who created you; from the time you were born, I have helped you. Do not be afraid' (Isa. 44:2, GNB).

My eyes filled with tears. I clearly felt the strong presence of God's living Spirit coming that afternoon to guide me, a lost sheep.

Prayer: *O God, help us to remember that you love us. Give us strength to pray when times get rough. Help us to remember that you are the Good Shepherd, always caring for your sheep. Amen.*

Thought for the Day: God never forgets us.

EinarIngvi Magnusson (Bratislava, Slovakia)

PRAYER FOCUS: THOSE WHO HAVE ABANDONED GOD   147

Careful Focus

Read Nehemiah 2:17-20 and 6:9, 15-16
The gracious hand of my God [was] upon me. Nehemiah 2:18 (NIV)

I kept fretting over the persistent pain in my hands. Housework, weeding the garden and even helping my children dress caused my hands to scream in protest. When I tried to spend time with God, I found myself thinking about the pain instead.

At the time, I was reading the book of Nehemiah. This man who loved God was striving to rebuild the wall around God's city, Jerusalem. Nehemiah rallied hundreds to help. Throughout the massive project, Nehemiah prayed and then depended on God for success. Amazingly, in just 52 days the new wall was completed. Everyone knew it was a work of God.

During the rebuilding process, enemies of Israel threatened and taunted God's people, trying to intimidate the workers. They shouted, 'Their hands will get too weak for the work, and it will not be completed.' Nehemiah wasn't distracted by their attempts at intimidation. Instead he prayed, 'Now strengthen my hands' (Neh. 6:9, NIV).

As I read Nehemiah's prayer, I realised my focus was badly misplaced. Nehemiah's life reminded me to pray despite obstacles. I adjusted my focus. Depending on God, I chose to watch for God's power in my life.

Prayer: *Thank you, God, for always hearing our prayers. Give us your strength for today. Amen.*

Thought for the Day: God's strength comes to us one day at a time.

Linda Watson (Illinois)

Painting God

1 Corinthians 2:6-16
Trust in the LORD with all your heart and lean not on your own understanding. Proverbs 3:5 (NIV)

My grandmother is a talented artist. She has 12 grandchildren, and we all had our turn in her studio to see if we inherited her gift. I soon realised that my talents lie elsewhere. As hard as I tried, I could never make my painting look real, as Grandma's did. My attempts at art looked more like cartoons. She told me that I should pay attention to what I was seeing and draw that, not what I thought my subject should look like. Although I never caught on to painting, Grandma did teach me a lesson about God.

I spent many years 'painting' God as I thought God should be. Because I could not understand some things about God, I made up my own image. Like my paintings, the end result was pretty pathetic. And when times got hard for me, my hope crumbled. But my grandmother's advice has helped me in my Christian walk. It has helped me to let go of what I thought God should look like and look to the Bible to see what God is really like.

Prayer: *Perfect Father, you reveal yourself to us through your word. Help us to seek your face.* Amen.*

Thought for the Day: Based on your favourite Bible passage, what is God like?

Sarah Negori (Louisiana)

PRAYER FOCUS: ARTISTS

149

*See Psalm 27:8

Miseries of the Rich

Read Matthew 6:19-24

Do not forget to do good and to share with others, for with such sacrifices God is pleased. Hebrews 13:16 (NIV)

An intelligent and industrious young man in my village secured a good job in Kuwait, worked hard and earned a lot of money within a short time. On his return to the village, he established a private bank and opened a jewellery shop. Many people deposited their money in his bank, and his business flourished.

But one morning people found his bank and shop closed indefinitely. Fearing for the fate of their deposits, they complained to the police, and eventually the young man was found and arrested. Then it was revealed that he had invested all the bank's money in doubtful business ventures in order to make a quick profit. When these failed, he lost everything. Finally he was imprisoned and all his properties confiscated.

In today's scripture reading, Jesus tells us that we should not focus our attention on wealth and warns us against wrong attitudes towards wealth. When we allow possessions to control us, we travel a slippery path that leads to destruction. But if we place ourselves and our wealth in God's hands, these can bless others, and our wealth will contribute to the welfare of the wider community.

Prayer: *Source of all good, make us aware that wealth is transient. Help us store up riches in heaven by doing your will on earth. Amen.*

Thought for the Day: God invites us to use what we have for the good of others.

T.V. John (Kerala, India)

A Land of Exile

Read 2 Corinthians 1:3-7

Praise be to the God and Father of our Lord Jesus Christ, the Father of compassion and the God of all comfort, who comforts us in all our troubles. 2 Corinthians 1:3-4 (NIV)

The death of my only son cast me into exile in a country filled with empty places — places of sadness and loss. I realised that I would never see him marry, have children or pursue his dreams.

As I have walked this path of sorrow, my journey has intersected with the paths of others whose children have died. We have shared memories of our beloved children; we have wept and prayed together. We have forged a bond that builds encouragement and provides comfort that cannot be found in any other place. Now the tears that once came from raw anguish have begun to flow in a new form, softened by the comfort and healing that has come over time.

Other mothers who have walked this same path have offered their time and love to help me find a 'new normal' for facing daily tasks. In turn, I have been strengthened to give the same love to newly exiled women who cross my path. My prayer time now includes my cry for their time in exile, in their empty places. My healing in this land of exile has brought opportunity to offer support and comfort to others.

Prayer: *Lord, equip us to bring your peace and comfort to those who walk in exile. Amen.*

Thought for the Day: Praying for another's healing helps to heal us.

Janet Huff (Illinois)

PRAYER FOCUS: SUPPORT GROUPS FOR THOSE GRIEVING

Today's Worries

Read Matthew 6:25-34

Do not worry about tomorrow, for tomorrow will worry about itself.
Matthew 6:34 (NIV)

In my garden are several bird feeders that I try to keep full of seeds. Sometimes when I return from travelling or run out of feed, I notice that no birds come near the feeders. Sometimes I worry and feel guilty that I have let the food run out. But as soon as I fill the feeders, within hours the usual assortment of birds finds its way back. I wonder who takes care of the birds when I cannot.

In a similar way, when my son's Boy Scout troop collects tinned food for the hungry, I worry that as much as we give, it never seems to be enough. When I think about how many people go hungry or need to hear God's word each day, the challenge seems overwhelming. There will always be more than we alone can do. What is the answer?

Christ tells us to put our faith in God. To be concerned is a call to action, but that does not mean a call to worry. Instead, we do what we can with what God puts at our disposal, and we trust God to take care of the rest (see 1 Cor. 3:6-8).

Prayer: *Dear God, remind us to share what you give us with those in need and then to be still, waiting for your will to be done. Amen.*

Thought for the Day: Long after we've done all we can, God will still be working.

Mark H. Anderson (Pennsylvania)

Checking the Fence

Read Psalm 119:97-106

All scripture is inspired by God and is useful for teaching, for reproof, for correction, and for training in righteousness, so that everyone who belongs to God may be proficient, equipped for every good work.
2 Timothy 3:16 (NRSV)

Many mornings on my way to work, I see two farmers carefully checking their fence, which borders a busy road. They make sure the posts are secure and the wire is intact to keep their cattle safe from the dangers of the road and from wandering onto property that doesn't belong to the farmers. Their diligence is necessary, since many times I see cattle leaning over the wire trying to snatch a mouthful of grass or to satisfy their curiosity. Without that fence, the cattle would wander.

In many ways, God's word is like that fence. The Bible tells me how to set safe boundaries in my life to keep me from the dangers of sinful actions and bad decisions. Whatever the day brings, God's word offers me the answers I need for living that day. But, like the ranchers, I need to 'check my fence' daily. Some days I don't want to hear from God's word because I'm leaning on the wire trying to go my own way. But daily Bible reading keeps my spiritual fence in good repair and helps me remain in God's safe pasture.

Prayer: *Heavenly Father, thank you for the power, practicality and truth of your word. Help us to be faithful in reading it and doing what is right as we seek to honour you in all things. Amen.*

Thought for the Day: Daily Bible reading helps to keep us where God wants us to be.

Laurinda Wallace (Arizona)

Seen or Unseen

Read Daniel 12:1-13

At that time Michael, the great prince, the protector of your people, shall arise. There shall be a time of anguish… But at that time your people shall be delivered, everyone who is found written in the book.
Daniel 12:1 (NRSV)

As winter approaches, the sky is darker and darker when my beagle gets me up for a walk every morning. Usually, many stars shine brightly in the darkness, giving me something to enjoy and praise God for even as I shiver in the rural cold.

But for a week recently, cloud cover hid the stars from view. I resented this especially because I wanted to see the pretty conjunction of the waning moon and the planet Mercury. Then I realised that whether or not I could see it, the great drama of the night sky would still go on. I don't have to see it to know it is happening.

Today's reading from Daniel seeks to reassure a persecuted people by reminding them — and us — of the truth that whether or not we can see it, a great drama is going on that is every bit as real as the stars in the sky. The archangel Michael is described as 'the protector of [God's] people'. Because of this reality, we can rest assured that God's story is being played out, seen or unseen. Whether we realise it or not, God is at work.

Prayer: *God of the stars, protect us and deliver us, we pray. Amen.*

Thought for the Day: God's power is as real as the heavens, and all will be well.

Frank Ramirez (Pennsylvania

A Nurtured Seed

Read 1 Peter 1:13-25

If anyone is in Christ, there is a new creation: everything old has passed away; see, everything has become new! 2 Corinthians 5:17 (NRSV)

I was a lost soul the first time I spoke with a pastor. Our conversation was not about spiritual matters; it was about me meeting the community-service obligation of my court sentence. Because I was pregnant, he offered to count the hours I spent attending church services towards my obligation, rather than requiring me to perform physical labour.

Initially, I sat in the rear of the church, counting down the minutes to freedom. As time passed, however, I started listening to the sermons. The words began speaking to my heart and tugging at my soul. The pastor knew that faith comes by hearing the word of God (see Rom. 10:17). Eventually, I found my way to the altar to accept Christ as my Saviour. During those moments I knelt at the altar, a seed of faith was planted within my heart.

Since then the Holy Spirit and the word of God have nurtured that seed. I feel transformed from the inside out. As my faith grew, so did my desire to repent and to change my ways. Today I am no longer lost. I'm safe and secure in God's love.

Prayer: *Thank you, Lord Jesus, for saving us. Thank you for the Holy Spirit who guides and helps us to grow. Keep us close to you as we live our faith day by day. In your holy name we pray. Amen.*

Thought for the Day: How has God transformed me from the inside out?

Giovanna Justus (Ohio)

Two Speed Bumps and a Left Turn

Read Acts 16:25-34

To all who received him, who believed in his name, he gave power to become children of God. John 1:12 (NRSV)

I always hesitate to ask directions. Some people give great directions — but some don't. Faulty directions can get us lost, be inconvenient, and sometimes be dangerous. However, even good directions must be listened to carefully. Recently, directions from a friend of mine proved helpful, even unique. Karen told me the main streets leading to her sister Judy's house. 'Then,' she said, 'it's just two speed bumps and a left turn!' I laughed. But I followed those instructions, and sure enough, I arrived safely at Judy's front door.

God has given us clear, concise directions that lead us to eternal life. If we listen and believe, God will lead us to our eternal home. The Bible tells us that the way is through Jesus Christ. The way will not be smooth. We're sure to encounter bumps, perhaps even go through dark valleys, but ultimately following Christ will lead us home.

Prayer: *Lord, grant us ears to hear and the will to obey, as we pray, 'Our Father which art in heaven, Hallowed be thy name. Thy kingdom come. Thy will be done, as in heaven, so in earth. Give us day by day our daily bread. And forgive us our sins; for we also forgive every one that is indebted to us. And lead us not into temptation; but deliver us from evil.'** Amen.

Thought for the Day: If we faithfully follow God's direction, we will not lose our way.

Patsy J. Dobson (Kansas)

A Thankful Heart

Read Ephesians 1:3-14

In every thing give thanks for this is the will of God in Christ Jesus concerning you. 1 Thessalonians 5:18 (KJV)

One day last week I awoke thinking of things I wanted but didn't have. My first impulse was to complain; then I decided to write down all the things I had to be thankful for. It wasn't long until I had a list that filled several pages.

When I thought of the many blessings God has given me through Christ, joy rose in my heart. I could sense the presence of God with me. I no longer felt sorry for myself. The temptation to complain about my life had vanished. Tears of gratitude formed in my eyes as I reflected on all the wonderful things God has given me.

I am grateful that God wants a relationship with me and calls me a son. Through reading God's word, I find many reasons to be thankful. When I focus on all the good things in my life, God's great love for me becomes real. Now when I am tempted to complain, I get out my list and review all that I have to be thankful for. Then all other concerns are by comparison insignificant.

Prayer: *O Lord, help us to see all of your goodness to us. May we remind others of your goodness and love. Amen.*

Thought for the Day: What do I have to be thankful for?

James Howard (Florida)

The Good Shepherd

Read Ezekiel 34:20-31
He is our God, and we are the people of his pasture, and the sheep of his hand. Psalm 95:7 (NRSV)

We enjoy living at the edge of town. One night, my husband and I were sitting in our living room when we heard a little tap, tap, tap on our porch. My husband turned on the porch light and opened the door. Imagine his surprise to see seven sheep all in a row!

He went round the porch to the garden, thinking he would herd them into a safe place until he could find their owner. They followed him; and when he opened the gate, they went in, one by one. Everywhere he went, they went too. Those sheep might have fallen prey to predators that roam in our area if they had not depended on my husband. For a while, he became their shepherd. The next day, he found the sheep's owner; but to tell the truth, he missed them when they left.

We are like those lost sheep. Without a shepherd, we wander in our own little world at risk of falling prey to temptation and harm. We all need a shepherd who leads us to 'green pastures' and 'still waters' (Ps. 23:2). Without a shepherd, sheep are in danger. Without the Good Shepherd, so are we.

Prayer: *Dear Lord, thank you for being our shepherd, guiding us through this life with love. Amen.*

Thought for the Day: When we become lost, our Good Shepherd searches for us.

Joan Clayton (New Mexico)

Speak Softly

Read Proverbs 15:1-4

A soft answer turns away wrath, but a harsh word stirs up anger.
Proverbs 15:1 (NRSV)

Recently an incident in my workplace caused a misunderstanding between me and one of my colleagues and we argued. She at once stopped talking to me. My first thought was to treat her in the same way, but then I remembered the verse, 'A soft answer turns away wrath.' At once I prayed silently, asking God to give me grace in this situation. I continued to talk with her and offered her help whenever she required it. Slowly she started speaking with me in her usual cheerful manner, and soon the small tiff was forgotten.

I was happy that I listened to the Spirit's guidance and applied the words of scripture to my life. Whatever our circumstances, if we trust in God and put the wisdom of scripture into practice, the Lord is able to work everything out for our good. God can give us grace to be loving even in times of disagreement. Treating others kindly also sets an example for those around us. Perhaps by doing so we can help them to realise the true meaning of Christianity.

Prayer: *Lord, give us grace to live in Christ-like ways so that we bring others to you by our example. Amen.*

Thought for the Day: Christ calls us to love even those with whom we disagree.

Anna Alex (Safat, Kuwait)

Advent of Hope

Read John 1:6-8, 19-28; 1 Thessalonians 5:16-24
Jesus said, 'The Spirit of the Lord is upon me, because he has anointed me to bring good news.' Luke 4:18 (NRSV)

The season of Advent lays the foundation for the celebration of Christmas. Luke tells us in his Gospel (4:16-21) that Jesus proclaimed himself the fulfilment of the promise God made to restore the people (see Isa. 61:1-4). This is our hope. This is what we look forward to in the birth of the Christ Child. In the meantime, we enter into a time of expectation, a season pregnant with what is to come.

The scriptures lead and counsel us on how to receive again the Gift of Love that is to be born. In 1 Thessalonians 5:16-24 Paul tells a faithful community how to live expectantly: to rejoice and pray, to give thanks in everything, to cling to the good and reject evil. It is good counsel for us in Advent.

We have become a part of a sacred history, and we are called to live responsibly — faithful to the purposes of God. In Advent we have an opportunity to prepare to receive the Christ anew in our lives, refreshing and restoring our faith with ancient truth and future hope.

Prayer: *O God, make us ready to welcome, in the birth of the Christ Child, the hope and purposes of your vision. Amen.*

Thought for the Day: Jesus is the Light of the world which no darkness can overcome.

F. Richard Garland (Rhode Island)

A Christmas Joy

Read Mark 12:41-44

[Jesus] called his disciples and said to them, 'Truly I tell you, this poor widow has put in more than all those who are contributing to the treasury.' Mark 12:43 (NRSV)

For many years one of my Christmas joys has been helping the Salvation Army by standing outside in a shopping centre with a collection box. Some days the winter cold make this challenging and unpleasant, but the faces of the people who give money make it all worthwhile. Last Christmas season a dear elderly lady stood near me searching a long time in her purse for some elusive coins. She looked as if she were the one who needed financial help. Finally, she beamed with success as she put her meagre offering into the box. As Jesus noted in his story of the widow and her penny, it was the sacrificial giving from the heart that mattered.

Often during my Salvation Army collecting experience, I notice that the people who give the most are often the ones who seem to be the poorest, and their beaming countenance reflects their gift. But the ones I remember the most are the children who deposit coins given to them by a parent. When they hear the words 'Merry Christmas' they flash the most wonderful smiles. Yes, giving — however small the amount — can bring us a bright face and a soaring spirit.

Prayer: *O God, we know you ask us to be cheerful givers. We pray our humble gifts bring joy to others. Amen.*

Thought for the Day: The joy of giving cannot be hidden!

Jack Ballard (Colorado)

Who Shut the Door?

Read Genesis 7

They went into the ark with Noah, two and two of all flesh in which there was the breath of life. And those that entered, male and female of all flesh, went in as God had commanded him; and the LORD shut him in.
Genesis 7:15-16 (NRSV)

Who closed the ark's door before the torrential rains began? My daughter, Katie, noticed that God shut the door. Her comments shed light on the scripture. Then she also reminded me that I follow a bedtime ritual: I go downstairs and make sure all the doors of our home are shut and locked. I check to make sure all the lights are out. As Katie drifts off to sleep, she feels safe and secure because she knows her daddy is watching, making sure that the doors are locked and that she is safe inside. 'God wanted Noah to feel safe before the awful storm,' she remarked, 'so God did a check and locked the door for Noah.'

I had heard the story of Noah many times and had never given this little verse much thought. Was God trying to make Noah feel safe? Katie thinks so.

One thing is certain: God closed the door out of love for Noah. As we approach storms in our lives, God loves us with the same great capacity and looks out for us with the same sensitive care.

Prayer: *God, remind us that your love constantly watches out for us. Amen.*

Thought for the Day: How do I see God's care in my life?

Tom Smith (Utah)

All Over the World

Read Psalm 112
[The righteous] are not afraid of evil tidings; their hearts are firm, secure in the Lord. Psalm 112:7 (NRSV)

Listening to news reports about war, terrorism and natural disasters, we may find life disturbing. Added to these, news of theft, murder, deception, child abuse and pornography bombards our minds. We can only wonder why God has not given up on humanity.

Then, we pick up *The Upper Room* daily devotional. As we glance through our copy of this little book, we see writings from Christians all over the world. We do not have to feel discouraged and frightened; we are surrounded by a vast Christian family. I find comfort in knowing that Jesus Christ still lives in the hearts of people everywhere and that believers all around the world see God at work where they are.

Our world is huge, but our Christian family is only a prayer away. After reading *The Upper Room* meditation each day, I pray for the writer and the writer's family and community. What a comfort to know that God's people are connected even in these disturbing times!

Prayer: *Lord, thank you for those who remind us of your presence and work. Amen.*

Thought for the Day: In these pages, Christians all over the world remind us that God is alive and well and working on planet Earth.

Marta Strong (North Carolina)

Grace for All

Read Romans 5:6-17

While we were still weak, at the right time Christ died for the ungodly.
Romans 5:6 (NRSV)

We took our young children to a farm nearby looking for a Christmas tree. The huge farm was unkempt, having been neglected over many years. The trees were overgrown and had been picked over for years, so only the less desirable ones were left.

Walking over the farm, we saw trees that were crooked, at the end of their strength and full of dead limbs. Others were poorly shaped, infected with insects, and had trunks too large for the tree holder. As we continued to search for a suitable tree, I overheard a young woman tell her husband, 'I have never seen so many trees with something wrong with them!'

This statement reminded me of a contrast. While families desire a near-perfect tree at Christmas, Christ accepts us as we are, warts and all. Christ is not particular. He welcomes the poor, the disabled, the downtrodden. He embraces thieves, abusers and sinners of all descriptions. It's hard to disqualify for Christ's love. His grace and forgiveness is available to all — if we only ask.

Prayer: *Strengthen my faith, loving God, as I rely on your grace. Amen.*

Thought for the Day: Share your understanding of God's grace.

Roy B. Shave (Missouri)

Who's in Control?

Read Proverbs 3:1-6

Let me hear of your steadfast love in the morning, for in you I put my trust. Teach me the way I should go, for to you I lift up my soul.
Psalm 143:8 (NRSV)

Sometimes we try to act as if we are God. We begin to believe we can control our world and what goes on in it. Sometimes it takes a major change in our lives to make us realise we are not in control. A death in the family, a divorce or a serious illness shakes us loose from our delusion of power.

For me it was a heart attack and bypass surgery at the age of 42. Until then, I had given myself credit for my accomplishments: being the first in my family to graduate from college, obtaining a good job, buying a home. But I learned during my illness that I am not in control, and that only by letting go and accepting God's guidance would I truly be a disciple of Christ. I made the decision to live that way, and I now give God praise and credit for my accomplishments.

Life has new meaning for me. I still fall back into my old ways, but I don't stay there long. My daily reading of *The Upper Room* and time in prayer, giving thanks and seeking God's will, allow me to 'let go' again. I don't have to try to control the world any longer. I leave that to God.

Prayer: *Heavenly Father, show us what you want for us, and give us wisdom to do your will and not our own. In Jesus' name we pray. Amen.*

Thought for the Day: Where do I need to give up trying to control the world and let God be God?

Gary Dowdy (Tennessee)

PRAYER FOCUS: THOSE RECOVERING FROM SURGERY

Plenty for All

Read John 10:7-10

Look at the birds of the air; they do not sow or reap or store away in barns, and yet your heavenly Father feeds them. Are you not much more valuable than they? Matthew 6:26 (NIV)

Shortly after moving in, our new neighbours put several bird feeders on a tree at the edge of their garden. I can easily observe the tree from my bedroom window.

At dawn each day, birds of all sizes and colours flock to the feeders. They frantically flap their wings, each one seeking a perch that allows it to reach the food. Although our neighbours supply abundant food, the birds vigorously push each other out of the way to get to the bounty.

As I lie in bed and observe this daily ritual, the words of Jesus come to mind. 'Look at the birds of the air; they do not sow or reap or store away in barns, and yet your heavenly Father feeds them.' At the same time, I remember that God's hand also provides our food. I am grateful to live in a country with an abundance of food, but others live where food is scarce.

God is indeed the great provider and has given us food sufficient for all. The birds follow their instincts and push one another aside, but we who follow Jesus Christ can choose to share what God has given us.

Prayer: *Giver of all good gifts, give us compassion and generosity toward the hungry and homeless in our world. Amen.*

Thought for the Day: Our abundance can supply another's need.

Thelma Robinson (Nottinghamshire, England)

Wait Simply

Read Romans 13:11-14
You know what time it is, how it is now the moment for you to wake from sleep. Romans 13:11 (NRSV)

As a pastor, every Advent I tell people, 'Over the ages, Christians have found it a beneficial discipline to simply wait; to wait simply; and while they're waiting, to take an inventory of their lives.' And then people tell me, 'Don't be such a party-pooper.'

Yet we are called to prepare for Christ's coming as we wait. We prepare for Jesus' coming by acknowledging our need for him. Realising that we need Jesus isn't very merry. It requires us to be honest about what's missing in our lives and about what's wrong with us. Advent calls us to recognise that the void in our soul cannot be filled by gadgets, entertainment, food, alcohol, drugs, sports, busyness, travel, work, religion or church. We know that, because we've tried. These do not satisfy because the void in us is a God-shaped hole that only the Holy One can fill.

Advent prepares us to see that Jesus, the baby in the manger, is the Holy One of God. If we do not wake up, our sleepy eyes will not recognise God in the baby who looks more like us than like God.

Prayer: *Dear God, we have a habit of getting lost. As you wait for us to come home, teach us to wait for you to show us the way. Amen.*

Thought for the Day: In Christ God has given us the gift we most need.

Mike Ripski (Tennessee)

Say Thank You

Read Psalm 104:24-28

O LORD… the earth is full of your creatures… when you open your hand, they are filled with good things. Psalm 104:24, 27 (NRSV)

During the World Environment Conference, three unusual objects will be placed on the altar at many religious services in Denmark: a stone, an ear of corn and a fragment of a coral reef. The stones come from Greenland; the maize from Malawi; and the coral from the Pacific. These remind us that climate change caused by our behaviour affects people around the world.

Global warming has raised Greenland's ocean temperature, causing fish to disappear and making it impossible for many to feed their families. Maize represents the drought causing poor Malawian peasants to starve. Coral reminds us of the Pacific Ocean islands inundated because of ocean rise; families have lost everything and fled.

God gave us places to live, farm and fish, but our acts are destroying them and people's lives. Greed and consumerism are sin, and this throwaway mentality infects our dealings with each other. We think we can use and discard humans. But Jesus taught us to consider others our brothers and sisters and to see the world as our precious gift from God.

Prayer: *Generous God, thank you for your rich gifts that allow all of us to live. Help us honour our shared planet and each other. Amen.*

Thought for the Day: God created Earth to sustain us; we changed that.

Anders Gadegaard (Copenhagen, Denmark)

Patience

Read Ephesians 4:31-5:2
Those with good sense are slow to anger, and it is their glory to overlook an offence. Proverbs 19:11 (NRSV)

I stopped at the bank on my way home from work. My mind swirled with thoughts of all I had to do that evening: make dinner, finish the laundry, attend netball practice, mark papers. As I stepped up to the assistant at the counter and passed the deposit slip to her, she threw it back at me, saying, 'What do you think I am, a mind reader?' I had neglected to fill in my account information.

My first reaction was to ask to speak to the manager, but something about the look in her face stopped me. In the past, she had helped me in a friendly and efficient manner. So instead, I asked, 'Are you having a bad day?'

At this she burst into tears and said, 'My daughter had an operation today, and I couldn't be with her; I couldn't get the time off.' I reached my hand across the counter and held hers while she cried. From then on when I came into the bank, she always said, 'This is my customer.' I learned her name, and she told me that her daughter had recovered from her illness.

I know that God had intervened. If I had reported her, she might have lost her job. God gave me patience and taught me a lesson in compassion that day.

Prayer: *Dear God, help us to realise that those who are in pain need our compassion. Amen.*

Thought for the Day: Those who cannot be patient are often concealing great pain.

Ann V. Ingalls (Missouri)

Widows and Orphans

Read James 1:22-27
Religion that is pure and undefiled before God, the Father, is this: to care for orphans and widows in their distress, and to keep oneself unstained by the world. James 1:27 (NRSV)

While I was in foster care, in the home of a minister, my friends taunted me by saying that my mum would never return to get me. But they were wrong. She came for me after proving she could be a responsible adult by holding down a job and securing a place to live for her children.

As I was getting ready to leave his home, the minister spoke to my mum in private. I later found out that he had saved all the money he had received for my foster care. He gave it to my mum to help her make a fresh start. My foster dad was living out the truth of the scripture verse above.

But that verse from James goes much deeper in its meaning. An orphan is someone who has no living biological parents, but in a sense we are all spiritual orphans until we recognise God as our father. If we are to live 'pure and undefiled' religion, we must care for spiritual orphans by guiding them to relationship with our Father in heaven. My foster dad surely did, and my mum and I are living proof of the power of God to redeem broken lives through those who obey scripture's words.

Prayer: *Thank you, Father, that you make provision through your people to care for the orphans and widows of the world. Amen.*

Thought for the Day: God can use my acts of love to change someone's life.

Sandra Kay Ramirez (Ohio)

Sheep Who Are 'Heafed'

Read Ephesians 2:11-22

You were going astray like sheep, but now you have returned to the shepherd and guardian of your souls. 1 Peter 2:25 (NRSV)

Sheep roam over the hills in England's Lake District. Do they belong to someone? Ask a local shepherd, who will say, 'All the sheep on this side of the hill belong to me. They're a hardy breed. They stay out in all kinds of weather, and they find their food up in the hills. I bring them down for dipping, worming, lambing and shearing.'

'But what if they wander off?'

'They don't. They're heafed to my mountain.'

Heafed is a new word to me. Even without fences, these sheep know their own patch of ground. The mother sheep teach each generation of lambs where they belong.

I wandered far from God, because it is my nature to stray. But when I came to Jesus Christ, he 'heafed' me to himself. Now, when I am inclined to wander, the shepherd's voice speaks to my heart, calling me back.

Prayer: *Lord, we are glad that you are our shepherd. Help us; change our hearts so we never want to stray, as we pray, 'Our Father in heaven, hallowed be your name, your kingdom come, your will be done on earth as it is in heaven. Give us today our daily bread. Forgive us our debts, as we also have forgiven our debtors. And lead us not into temptation, but deliver us from the evil one.'* Amen.*

Thought for the Day: We are free to roam, but we can choose to stay close to Christ.

Marion Turnbull (Manchester, England)

PRAYER FOCUS: THOSE WANDERING FROM CHRIST
*Matthew 6:9-13 (NIV)

A Most Unlikely Gift

Read Isaiah 53:2-5

How are they to call on one in whom they have not believed? And how are they to believe in one of whom they have never heard? And how are they to hear without someone to proclaim him? Romans 10:14 (NRSV)

One December day several years ago, my six-year-old daughter, Alisha, selected an unusual Christmas gift for my wife. It was a huge candy cane the size of a garden ornament. Alisha would not change her mind, despite my and her brother's insistence that she consider something else. When Christmas arrived, my wife opened her present from Alisha. I unwrapped my gift from Alisha, a box of chocolates. These were soon eaten.

Six months later, Alisha died.

Two thousand years ago, God sent us a gift, a poor child, laid in a manger, and surrounded by unlikely people and even animals. God's unlikely gift was Jesus. We still celebrate his strange and beautiful entry into our world that he came to save.

Each Christmas season as I look at the candy cane hanging in a place of prominence in our house, I remember that unlikely gifts can have great significance. Jesus truly is the best gift we can give or receive.

Prayer: *God, help us to remember you not only on Christmas Day but on every day as we interact with other people. Amen.*

Thought for the Day: We have the privilege and responsibility to offer others the gift of faith in Christ.

Aaron Swavely (Pennsylvania)

Not Perfect

Read Titus 3:3-7

To him who is able to keep you from falling and to present you before his glorious presence without fault and with great joy... be glory, majesty, power and authority. Jude 24-25 (NIV)

During the holiday season, I sat down and put together a 1000-piece jigsaw puzzle. I took pleasure in assembling the colours and pictures to resemble the image on the box. To my dismay, when I was trying to finish my puzzle, I discovered that one piece was missing. The puzzle was flawed. I was so disappointed that I was ready to throw it away, to abandon the puzzle, and to start another one. But then I looked at it again and decided to keep it. It was still a beautiful picture, and I was not going to throw it away because it was not perfect.

I think God sees us in the same way. Each of us has the potential to become who God intends us to be, but we come up short. I am thankful that when I sin or fall short of God's hopes and expectations, God does not become discouraged and abandon me. We are all flawed. Thanks be to God, who still sees our value and refuses to throw us aside. Rather, God saves us through Jesus Christ!

Prayer: *Loving God, thank you for overlooking our flaws and for loving us despite our shortcomings. Amen.*

Thought for the Day: Serving God is one way we show our gratitude for God's unconditional love.

Robert L. Sandifer (Kansas)

PRAYER FOCUS: THOSE WHO FEEL INADEQUATE

The Best News

Read Romans 10:4-17

The angel said to them, 'Do not be afraid. I bring you good news of great joy that will be for all the people. Today... a Saviour has been born to you; he is Christ the Lord.' Luke 2:10-11 (NIV)

As we wait for the celebration of the coming of the Christ child, I reflect on what it means to celebrate Christmas. In our house we read our church's annual Advent devotional booklet as part of our daily dinner routine.

In Luke's account of Jesus' birth, we read about an angel who announced: 'Do not be afraid.' I, like the shepherds, would certainly need this reassurance. 'I bring you good news', the angel continued. Not only is this good news, it's the best news ever. My Saviour was born! Even if I were the only person on the face of the earth, God loved me enough to give me my own Saviour. The angel also mentioned 'great joy'. And this joy is for all the people of the world.

Our challenge is to be an announcing angel for everyone within our reach. With God's help, we can carry this joyful message by inviting a friend, neighbour or loved one to church; by phoning someone we haven't talked to for a long time; or by buying coffee or a meal for a homeless person. We have the best news that has ever been proclaimed: 'Your Saviour, your Christ, your Lord has been born!'

Prayer: *Father God, help us to take the best message ever to everyone we meet. In Jesus' name we pray. Amen.*

Thought for the Day: Share the best news!

Christine Kalmbach (Texas)

Wherever God Is

Read Matthew 25:34-40

Jesus said, 'It is not the healthy who need a doctor, but the sick. I have not come to call the righteous, but sinners to repentance.' Luke 5:31-32 (NIV)

The establishment has a reputation — a bad one. Every so often the police raid the premises, and in the paper we read often of arrests being made there. No respectable person ever goes there, and in the evening it is not wise even to walk past the door.

One day during daylight hours I was walking by on the other side of the road and happened to look up. There, growing out of the side of the chimney of the building, was a lush green plant with a deep red flower. Obviously some soil was lodged up there, and God, the creator of all that is good, was gracing this place with a token of nature's beauty.

It made me think about where God is. Some places we avoid; we do not want to become contaminated. But God has no such reservations. God is lying beside the homeless on the bitter cold nights, beside prisoners in their solitary cells and beside the drug addicts in their addiction. Surely where God is, we should be also.

Prayer: *Lord, may we go where you want us to go, speak to those you want us to speak to, and pray and speak for those who do not have a voice. Amen.*

Thought for the Day: God is at work in places I would never go.

Carol Purves (Cumbria, England)

PRAYER FOCUS: THOSE I CONSIDER UNTOUCHABLE

What Should I Do?

Read Genesis 1:26-28
The LORD God took the man and put him in the garden of Eden to till it and keep it. Genesis 2:15 (NRSV)

When we face big challenges such as those happening with the environment, we may shrink back, blaming others rather than taking personal responsibility. Though the problems may be new, the Bible reminds us from its first chapters of the human tendency to shift blame (see Gen. 3:1-13).

Years ago I sat in a management meeting where we listed many tasks our community faced. We decided that our primary task was to create a good environment for our children. Afterwards, some of us stayed on for conversation. One of the participants brought up the subject of helping people who are ill, and talked about the challenge of encouraging those in difficult situations.

I told her about my experiences as a pastor with such visits and ended by saying, 'Usually it is I who am enriched by such a visit.'

'Yes,' she replied, 'but you have something to offer them!' This response gave me a lot to think about. As we face the world's environmental problems, believers can remember that God works with us as we tend the planet placed in our care.

Prayer: *Dear God, help me act today to care for your creation. Help each of us to realise that you want us to leave the world healthier than we found it. Amen.*

Thought for the Day: When we care for the earth, we do God's bidding.

Knut Bjarne Jorgensen (Vonge, Denmark)

Daddy's Church

Read Luke 2:41-51

[Jesus] said to them, 'Why were you searching for me? Did you not know that I must be in my Father's house?' Luke 2:49 (NRSV)

The whole family was strolling down the main street of our town, window-shopping and listening to Christmas carols sung or played by choirs and brass bands. After a while, we met one of the ladies from our church and stopped to chat.

Without our being aware of it, our three-year-old son, Harald, walked away to look at something interesting and became lost. We started shouting his name and began searching for him. After a short time, a woman approached us. Harald was walking beside her, holding her hand. 'I found him sobbing and thought I should take him to the police. But as we walked toward the police station, he suddenly pointed at a building and said, "Look! That's Daddy's church!" Then I understood who he belonged to. I had seen you walking in the town so I knew where to take him.'

Going astray is easy because many things take our focus away from the Lord. But when we find ourselves far from where we know God wants us to be, one landmark never fails. We belong to God. We will find our way home when we seek fellowship with those who follow Christ.

Prayer: *Dear Lord, keep us close so that we do not lose our direction in life. Amen.*

Thought for the Day: Even when we stray, we are God's beloved children.

Oystein Brinch (Oslo, Norway)

God's Great Gift

Read Isaiah 9:2-7
A child has been born for us… and he is named … Prince of Peace.
Isaiah 9:6 (NRSV)

Last Christmas, my mother and I agreed not to give each other Christmas presents. Instead, we decided that we would enjoy the holiday by spending time together, going to church and visiting family. Besides saving money, Mother and I decided that we wanted to focus on the true spirit of Christmas.

As Christmas Day neared, it felt slightly odd not to be caught up in the shopping-buying-giving frenzy. Then I felt something stir inside me that was refreshing — and a bit startling. Instead of dwelling on what I could get Mother for Christmas, I reflected on how precious she and other family members are to me. Instead of competing with other shoppers for the best deal at the best price, I smiled more readily and was more available to hold a door open for a stranger. Instead of filling my hours with budget juggling and cost comparisons, I prayed for deeper gratitude and joy at the marvellous, wondrous gift God has given us in Jesus Christ.

On Christmas Day, Mother and I agreed that the holiday was our best yet — relaxed, inspiring and happy.

Prayer: *Help us, O God, to celebrate your gift of love by sharing it with others. Amen.*

Thought for the Day: What gifts of love can I give this Christmas?

Maureen Pratt (California)

Christ Living in Us

Read Titus 2:11-14

The grace of God brings salvation… teaches us to say 'No' to ungodliness and worldly passions, and to live self-controlled, upright and godly lives… while we wait for the… glorious appearing of our… Saviour, Jesus Christ. Titus 2:11-13 (NIV)

In preparation for the Christmas season our family members have baked and bought and wrapped and donated. We have also volunteered time with those in need. And we have put aside family differences to enjoy Christmas Day together.

Christmas is coming — time to unwrap the presents and enjoy a few precious days off work with family and friends. But is that all? When Titus writes of the appearing of our Lord Jesus Christ, his is not a let-down-your-hair message of celebration. Instead Titus speaks of renouncing impiety, of self-control, of redemption and zeal for good deeds.

We come together to celebrate the grace of God become flesh — a God who humbled himself to take the form of an infant. As we rejoice in the appearance of our Lord and Saviour, we are called to renounce our worldly passions and to seek redemption and purity — living godly lives for the least and the unwelcome in our communities. May our observances this year display to everyone around us not only our joy and generosity but also the purity and righteousness of Christ who lives in us.

Prayer: *God of life, transform my zeal for worldly goods into passion for your people and your world. Amen.*

Thought for the Day: We can rejoice by reflecting to others the righteousness and purity of Christ.

Kara Lassen Oliver (Tennessee)

PRAYER FOCUS: THAT OTHERS MAY SEE CHRIST IN US

Love in Person

Read 1 John 3:16-20

Dear children, let us not love with words or tongue but with actions and in truth. 1 John 3:18 (NIV)

Every year during the holidays, many people visit homeless shelters to serve the poor. If these servers are like me, they leave with soaring spirits and a new perspective on their material blessings. For years I was blessed to serve monthly dinner at a shelter, smiling and pouring drinks for the guests. But I needed more; I hungered for relationships with people in crisis.

I began worshipping at the shelter mid-day several times a week; we sang and prayed together, hugged and shared our pains. Through these encounters the Holy Spirit blessed me profoundly. These people are just like me, and they came to realise I was just like them. We are a family of believers and seekers with many of the same obstacles to faith and grace, though we look very different. We find great comfort in knowing we support one another through our daily trials.

During his short time in ministry, Christ called us to be humbled by our sins and weaknesses but also to put into action the gifts God has given us. We are to love our brothers and sisters as Jesus loved those in need — in person.

Prayer: *Heavenly Father, may the situations and people that break your heart, break our hearts. Amen.*

Thought for the Day: Love God's people — in person.

Dan Nelson (North Carolina)

I Am the Truth

Read John 1:1-18

Jesus said, 'I am the way, and the truth, and the life. No one comes to the Father except through me.' John 14:6 (NRSV)

A professor asked my college class, 'Why do people believe in God?' The students offered several reasons: 'People believe in God because they are afraid to die' or 'because they are uneducated' or 'because they are unaware of other options'. I remained silent, unnerved by what I had heard as hostile words from my classmates.

The professor listened carefully and then replied, 'Suppose people believe in God because it's true, because God is real.' His surprising response filled me inwardly with laughter and a sense of freedom.

Because we can trust that what the Bible says about God is true, we can face each day with joy, seeking to love and obey Christ. He speaks the truth and lives the truth; he is the Truth who sets us free (see John 8:32).

Prayer: *Lord Jesus, help us to love the truth and always to speak the truth in love.* May our lives and words reflect your truth and your love to others every day. As Jesus taught us, we pray, 'Our Father which art in heaven, Hallowed be thy name. Thy kingdom come. Thy will be done in earth, as it is in heaven. Give us this day our daily bread. And forgive us our debts, as we forgive our debtors. And lead us not into temptation, but deliver us from evil: For thine is the kingdom, and the power, and the glory, for ever. Amen.***

Thought for the Day: The Truth still sets us free.

Robert J. Phillips (Illinois)

PRAYER FOCUS: COLLEGE STUDENTS

*(See Ephesians 4:15) **Matthew 6:9-13 (KJV)

Loved at Last

Read Romans 8:9-16
You did not receive a spirit of slavery to fall back into fear, but you have received a spirit of adoption. When we cry, 'Abba! Father!' it is that very Spirit bearing witness with our Spirit that we are children of God.
Romans 8:15-16 (NRSV)

I am a victim of Shy-Drager Disease, and doctors have said I have only 10 years of life remaining. The increasing burden on my family is a great concern to me, but the peace in my heart and my trust in God is increasing daily.

From childhood, I was reared without the awareness of being loved. My parents appeared to love me, but I never felt their love. Even after I married, my heart was filled with anxiety and dissatisfaction. Severely troubled, I ran away into alcohol and thought about dying. While I was in that dark void, an encounter with the Bible brought a ray of light into my life. But still I was hesitant to accept God's love. Then when I became ill, every word of the Bible became real. I knew that I was a child of God, and I felt loved for the first time!

These days, though I am losing the use of my body little by little, I spend much of my time in prayer. I pray for my family and my church and for those throughout the world in poverty, that they might know God's help. While I still have life, I will pray and thank God for the precious gift of life on earth and life eternal.

Prayer: *Gracious God, many people are suffering in this world. Provide for their needs, that they may live in peace, and help us to bring your peace to them. Amen.*

Thought for the Day: What can I do for the Lord today?

Atsuko Sato (Kagoshima, Japan)

The Repairer

Read Isaiah 61:1-4

The LORD said, 'I will raise up the booth of David that is fallen, and repair its breaches, and raise up its ruins, and rebuild it. ... I will restore the fortunes of my people Israel, and they shall rebuild the ruined cities and inhabit them.' Amos 9: 11, 14 (NRSV)

Every Christmas Eve, my father would slip out of the house and head for the town. My sister and I never realised what he was doing until years later. Apparently, he was searching the stores for items he could repair or refurbish. Most shop owners were happy to make a little money on defective products, demonstration models, dismembered toys and such. My dad, always a good negotiator, whittled the prices down to almost nothing.

He would hide these soon-to-be Christmas gifts in the garage. After we had gone to bed, Dad would sneak out to his workshop, often staying up all night to mend the gifts. I never owned a completely new bicycle, toy car, or football boots; they were all second-hand items that Dad had reclaimed.

With an even more loving heart than my Dad's, God is also a repairer: of torn lives, splintered families and shattered hopes. All that causes us pain God yearns to heal.

Prayer: *Dear Lord, you have mended our lives so many times. Help us minister to others in the same way. Amen.*

Thought for the Day: What God restores becomes better than new.

Charles Harrel (Oregon)

PRAYER FOCUS: THOSE WHO ARE BROKENHEARTED

A Child is Born

Read Luke 2:1-20

[Mary] wrapped [the baby] in cloths and placed him in a manger, because there was no room for them at the inn. Luke 2:7 (NIV)

In an overcrowded train, dark and dirty beyond imagination, lay a woman in labour. Since I am a doctor, I could help. In a moment of silence, I prayed for help and guidance in what seemed an impossible situation. The baby was in breech; the mother was young and frail. The space around me was almost too small for me to move in it. But in a few minutes, a baby was born. What a joy! A child is born. Everyone in the coach chanted with joy in the African manner of celebrating the birth of a child.

On the night when Jesus was born in Bethlehem, Mary 'wrapped him in cloths and placed him in a manger because there was no room in the inn'. When Jesus was born, a great company of the heavenly host appeared with the angels to praise God. The birth of this child was good news for the whole world.

Christmas invites us to let Jesus be born in our lives. Then every day God will give us life, joy and peace.

Prayer: *Thank you, God, for the life of your Son and our king, Jesus Christ. Thank you, Immanuel, for the joy and peace you give us. Amen.*

Thought for the Day: No matter how dirty or crowded our situation may be, Christ can be born anew in our lives this Christmas.

Charlotte Mande Kasongbenge (Cape Town, South Africa)

Like Minds

Read Philippians 2:5-8

Let the same mind be in you that was in Christ Jesus.
Philippians 2:5 (NRSV)

Although they live hundreds of miles apart, my twin aunts remain deeply connected to one another. At times they seem to be of one mind, sending identical or very similar presents and cards to relatives. Each is so much like the other that many people cannot tell them apart.

How different the world would be if followers of Christ bore a striking resemblance to Jesus! Paul reminds us to align our minds, intellects and priorities with the thoughts and actions of Christ. In fact, if we live in unity with Christ, those watching us should catch a glimpse of Christ where they at first saw only us.

The path to oneness with Christ is not easy, and Paul uses challenging words to describe the journey. Christ, Paul says, 'emptied himself, taking the form of a slave… and became obedient to the point of death' (Phil. 2:7-8, NRSV). The message is clear: Union with Christ requires sacrifice, obedience and servanthood. Do we want to be like him?

Prayer: *Loving God, help us grow nearer to you this day. Change our hardened hearts and distracted minds so we may bear an ever-stronger resemblance to Christ Jesus. Amen.*

Thought for the Day: What one small thing can I do today to reflect Christ's presence in my life?

Donna E. Harris (North Carolina)

PRAYER FOCUS: FREEDOM FROM WORLDLY DISTRACTIONS

The Fourth Commandment

Read Mark 6:30-32
Six days you shall labour, but on the seventh day you shall rest.
Exodus 34:21 (NIV)

My parents' behaviour on most Sunday afternoons puzzled me. Why would they choose to waste time resting when there were so many things to do?

Not long after I married and started a family, I finally understood why God said, 'For six days, work is to be done, but the seventh day shall be your holy day, a Sabbath of rest to the Lord' (Exod. 35:2, NIV). God provided the Sabbath for worship and for rest. I now plan ahead to make certain I rest on Sunday afternoons after a morning at church.

Having a day to rest renews our energy and zest for life. A day to focus on something besides work also helps to prevent exhaustion. Jesus understood this need for rest. After the death of John the Baptist, Jesus told his disciples, 'Come with me by yourselves to a quiet place and get some rest' (Mark 6:31, NIV).

The Sabbath rest not only refreshes mind and body but also refreshes our spirit so that we can serve God more faithfully.

Prayer: *Dear Father, thank you for a day to spend special time with you in worship and in rest. Help us, God, to follow your example and to rest. Amen.*

Thought for the Day: Jesus needed rest, and so do we.

David A. Blanton (Texas)

Abundant Life

Read Isaiah 49:13-18

Jesus said, 'I came that they may have life, and have it abundantly.'
John 10:10 (NRSV)

The presents have been opened and the meals eaten; the house is a mess, and my family have gone. Because I spent weeks preparing for Christmas, I hardly know what to do now that my home is empty and quiet. Since it's only my third Christmas as a widow, I've yet to develop a way of coping with this void I feel.

Suddenly I'm aware of a familiar voice — the voice of the One who gave me weeks of grace while I buried myself in holiday preparations. Now, this voice whispers softly to me, 'I've come to bring you abundant life.' Human reason prompts me to argue, What's more abundant than a home filled with family at this time of year? God's answer comes before I can finish speaking. 'A heart filled with me lives in greater abundance.'

Of course family gatherings bring pleasure, but I've discovered lasting pleasure in spending time with God to receive comfort, wisdom and guidance. This abundance exists in a place that is open to each of us! Sadness and self-pity are easing now and loneliness is fading. I have no time for such things. I'm ready to live a truly abundant life.

Prayer: *O God, thank you for your love and presence that always surround us. Thank you for your wonderful gift of salvation and for the gift of abundant life now. In Jesus' name we pray. Amen.*

Thought for the Day: The abundant life that God offers can fill the greatest void.

Laura L. Bradford (Washington)

Against the Current

Read 1 John 5:1-5

Do not be conformed to this world, but be transformed by the renewing of your minds, so that you may discern what is the will of God.
Romans 12:2 (NRSV)

I was at the Niagara River surrounded by the beauty of God's creation. A kayak glided by, and I watched the kayaker's smooth, powerful strokes as he paddled against the current to head up river. What intrigued me was the current's incredible strength. It was amazing how fast it pulled along ducks and seagulls floating on the surface. Boats drifted randomly as the current twisted and turned.

It is hard to fight any current, especially the strong currents of our secular world. But the realm of faith is not about drifting along on the easy way of life; it's about following the call of God to places unknown. I thought about heroes of faith like Noah, who built an ark miles from any lake or river because God told him to, and Moses, who led a nation through the desert to the Promised Land.

It would be easy to follow the norm and go with the flow. But to do the work God calls us to do takes effort, perseverance, hope and vision. Faith sustains us as we make our way, even if it is against the current of life, to enter into the Promised Land.

Prayer: *O Lord, give us the courage and faith to follow wherever you lead. Strengthen us when the way is hard. Amen.*

Thought for the Day: Following Christ means going against our culture's ways.

Paul Emery (New York)

A New Identity

Read Isaiah 43:14-21

Do not remember the former things, or consider the things of old. I am about to do a new thing; now it springs forth, do you not perceive it?
Isaiah 43:18-19 (NRSV)

The thought of teaching English in a foreign country excited me, but I struggled with the reality of leaving my job and selling my furniture to strangers. Once I made the decision, however, I moved from my apartment to a temporary living arrangement with friends.

A few days before my departure, I sold my car. Then a strange thing happened: when I looked in my handbag, I didn't find any keys! These signs of my former identity — house key, office keys and car keys — were now in someone else's handbag or pocket. I felt a mixture of loss and freedom.

Then I realised that if I insist on holding on to the old or familiar, such as a comfortable job or a lifestyle, I may miss the new thing God desires for me. God is in the business of making things new. By God's grace, we have a new heart, a new spirit and a new identity. We have God's promise that we are becoming new creations in Christ. Old thoughts, motives and ways of viewing ourselves pass away. God plants in us new possibilities, new desires, and hope that does not disappoint us (see Rom. 5:5).

Prayer: *Dear God, give us the grace to let go of any and every thing that keeps us from new life in Christ. Amen.*

Thought for the Day: Every day, in some way, God is doing a 'new thing' in us.

Patricia Mohoney (Moscow, Russia)

The Daily Gift

Read Colossians 3:12-17

It is God's gift that all should eat and drink and take pleasure in all their toil. Ecclesiastes 3:13 (NRSV)

A local senior-citizens' centre held a New Year's Eve dance complete with decorations, food and a jukebox. The dancers were mostly in their 70s and 80s. One of them was less than graceful in his movements to the music, but he danced with all his heart while sporting a huge smile. When asked why he danced with such gusto, he replied that he did not know how many more days he would have to dance, laugh and enjoy himself — certainly not as many as he had already experienced.

I realised that none of us, regardless of our age, knows how many days we have left. The Bible tells us that while we are here our time is to be spent making disciples for Jesus Christ and being his witnesses, loving one another, praising God in all ways possible, living in peace and doing good.

How many days have I wasted in complaining, demanding my own way, withholding love and goodness? How many hours have gone by while I wallowed in self-pity, plotted revenge or pushed others aside? I cannot go back and retrieve those lost days and hours, but I can make the most of this day and every day that I have from now on.

Prayer: *Giver of Life, help us to live each day to glorify you. Amen.*

Thought for the Day: God wants us to enjoy life.

Brenda E. Shreve (West Virginia,

Small Group Questions

Wednesday 1 July, 2009

1. What would you say to someone who has just received bad news from a doctor? What are some things we might say in trying to be helpful that actually are not helpful? Would you respond differently to a non-believer than to a believer? Why or why not?

2. Recalling past experience, did facing a challenge initially bring you into a closer relationship with God or did it make you want to push away from God? Why?

3. Which type of suffering causes you the most struggle — physical, mental or emotional? Why do you suppose that is?

4. How do the members of your church act as 'angels' in the lives of the people in your community?

5. Can you recall a time when God 'put a new song in [your] mouth' (Ps. 40:3)? What were the circumstances? What was the 'new song'?

6. Besides health concerns, what would you say are people's top three or four subjects to worry about? Which scripture verses or stories offer help or wisdom about these common worries?

7. Is worrying a sin? Why or why not?

Wednesday 8 July, 2009

1. When have you found yourself too busy and feeling overloaded? What helps you regain balance when your life becomes lopsided?

2. When do you most need the affirmation of others? How do you cope or respond if you think you are not receiving that affirmation?

3. How can we decide when to say yes and when to say no to invitations to serve? Which people is it hard to say no to, and why? What motivates you to serve others or a cause voluntarily?

4. Is it bad to serve others for the 'wrong reasons', such as to gain affirmation? Should we serve others even when we don't want to? Why or why not?

5. What do you think causes 'spiritual unbalance'? What could help to correct it? Which Bible passages address this issue?

6. Read Luke 10:38-42 aloud and allow time to reflect on this question: What is 'the one thing needed' that Christ is pointing out to you? How will you respond to Christ's invitation?

Wednesday 15 July, 2009

1. Think of some subject, group of people or activity about which you have a very different perspective now than you did in times past. What was the subject, and what changed your ideas and response?

2. Who is the most effective Bible teacher you have known or heard? What makes or made that person an effective teacher?

3. When was the last time you saw something surprisingly new in a familiar Bible verse? What was the verse, and what was the insight? How did you come to it?

4. What does 'all Scripture is inspired by God' (2 Tim. 3:16) mean? Do you believe this? Which Bible verses or stories puzzle you or do you find difficult to accept or explain? Why?

5. What can we do regularly to help us look more closely at the Bible? What can help us to see familiar passages in new ways?

6. How does the quoted scripture, 2 Timothy 3:16-17, affect your daily life?

Wednesday 22 July, 2009

1. What is your biggest question about prayer?

2. How do you think prayer 'works'? Are some prayers more likely to be answered than others? Why do you say this?

3. This writer says that prayer is 'a mystery' yet he continues to pray. What mysteries have you decided to accept and live with, without giving up on God or your faith? How did you come to this acceptance?

4. When has praying changed you? How has it changed you?

5. What 'personal compulsion' are you willing to share with the group? Do you consider this compulsion a positive or negative in your life? Why?

6. Do you agree with the writer that 'Prayer is as much for me as it is for God'? How so? What do you think is 'in it' for God?

Wednesday 29 July, 2009

1. Thinking about your family and inserting your family surname in the blank, complete one of these sentences:

'The _____s are known for…'

'The _____s believe in…'

'The _____s have had (some occupation or talent) in every generation.'

3. If your neighbours were asked to describe you, what 'family characteristics' of Christians might they include? What family characteristics of Christians would you like them to include? Based on your recent interactions with them, would they be likely to do so?

4. Have you ever had the opportunity to see yourself as others see you?

If so, was the reflected image you saw welcome or unwelcome? What image does God's 'perfect law of liberty' reflect to you (Jas.1:23-25) about qualities and characteristics that you need to develop?

5. How would you answer the question posed in the Thought for the Day?

6. When have you experienced a situation when you would not (or were reluctant to) acknowledge to others that you are a Christian? Why do you think someone would not be willing to proclaim his or her faith in Christ?

Wednesday 5 August, 2009

1. Do you believe that Christians need to limit their possessions to necessities? How do you decide where to draw the line in spending your money? How might possessions interfere with following Christ?

2. To what degree do you believe that Jesus can 'fulfil all [your] needs and desires'? For what need do you find it most difficult to trust God to provide?

3. This story from Luke 18 says that the man 'went away sad, for he had many possessions'. Do you think the man was sad because he was going to do what Jesus told him to or because he was not going to do it?

4. People talk about 'traveling light' and 'living simply'. What do these phrases imply? What is it about their intent that you find attractive? What is it about them that you find worrying?

5. Take a mental tour of your home. What do you have more of than you need? How might your abundance be used to honour Christ?

5. When has God provided for you in a surprising way? Did you recognise God's hand at work at the time or only when looking back later?

Wednesday 12 August, 2009

1. What would you consider to be a 'roadblock' to your faith? What would it take to remove this roadblock?

2. Does your faith come mostly from your mind or your heart? How can reason help us in our faith? How can it be a barrier to faith? Why do people try to prove matters of faith?

3. What has helped you in times when you have struggled to believe? What can help us to live faithfully even when we are unsure of ourselves and our faith?

4. When is God most real to you? What reassures you of God's presence and care?

5. Consider the quoted scripture (Prov. 3:5) and/or Isaiah 55:9: Declares the Lord, 'As the heavens are higher than the earth, so are my ways higher than your ways and my thoughts than your thoughts' (NIV). Can you recall a specific truth of the Bible that goes against human reasoning and wisdom? When have you been able to discover the wisdom in one of God's 'unlikely' truths?

6. Recount an instance when you, like the father in Mark 9, both believed and didn't believe at the same time. Is doubt always bad? What did you learn from this period in your life?

Wednesday 19 August, 2009

1. Do you consider that a 'peacemaker' and a 'terrorist' are both made in God's image? Why or why not?

2. When have you seen Christ in someone not identified as Christian? Do you agree with the writer that this doctor was an agent of God's care for the people of Somalia? Why or why not?

3. What places in addition to Somalia might be described as 'God-forsaken'? How have you learned about them? How have you shown God's compassion towards their people?

4. What is our Christian obligation towards those suffering in other lands? Is it ever OK to ignore them? How do we avoid being overwhelmed by the huge problems of others?

5. Describe a time when you formed a negative opinion about an individual or a group, only to discover later that you were mistaken in your initial assessment. How did you come to a different conclusion? What made the difference?

6. Does God require us to take a side on every issue? How do we know when to be neutral and when to take corrective action? What does the Bible say about both responses? Is there another response? If so, what might that be?

Wednesday 26 August, 2009

1. When have you tried something new and had awful results? When have you tried something new and had good results? Could you have changed either outcome?

2. What first made you want a relationship with God? Have the reasons changed since then? How?

3. What motivates you to maintain your relationship with God? Is it more about your love for God or your fear of God? Why?

4. What evidence of God's goodness have you seen in your life this week? Did you identify this as God's goodness at the time?

5. What is the difference between knowing about God and knowing God? How can we help people move from knowing about God to knowing God? Is this move within our control? If not, how and why should we witness?

6. To what degree is this 'taste and see' verse an invitation to test God? How do we reconcile the many passages in which testing God is condemned (Deut. 6:16; Ps. 78:18, 41, 56; Ps. 106:14; Matt. 4:7; Lk. 4:12; etc.) with this passage and ones such and Malachi 3:10: '"Test me in this," says the LORD Almighty.'?

Wednesday 2 September, 2009

1. Do you relate to the way this writer applies the idea of multi-tasking to the way we sometimes approach our time with God? If so, in what way? If not, why not?

2. What are your 'hands' presently filled with when you come to God? What do you find difficult to offer God with 'both hands'? What 'worldly matter' do you find yourself clutching that distracts you and divides your attention?

3. What helps you focus all your attention on God? What do you need to change so that you worship God with all your heart and all your life?

4. In the quoted scripture, the psalmist sets up a goal: 'that I may fear your name'. What role does fear play in our relationship with God?

5. How is the worship of your community of faith focused on God? In what ways does your church community offer God a divided heart?

6. How can you help your faith community to come before God united, with an undivided heart?

7. What do you consider to be the primary focus and intent of worship? How does this differ from other approaches you have observed?

Wednesday 9 September, 2009

1. Describe a time when you felt unlovable in some way. What impact did this period have on the rest of your life? What did you learn from it?

2. Who has shown you the love of God? How were you changed as a result?

3. Think about a person you tend to avoid. How would Jesus respond in the same situation? What specific actions could you take to alter your response?

4. When have you turned away from other people because they were physically disfigured or socially unacceptable?

5. What area of human suffering touches your heart the most? What are you doing to relieve those who suffer in this way?

6. In what ways can your community of faith show the love of God to people who are physically disfigured or socially unacceptable?

Wednesday 16 September, 2009

1. What do 1 Timothy 4:11-16 and 2 Timothy 3:14-15 say about the Bible?

2. What does your church teach about the Bible? What do you believe about the Bible?

3. When you were a child, who read to you from the Bible? Who taught you the meaning of scripture? From whom did you learn the beliefs of Christian faith?

4. What motivates you to read or study the Bible? Do you usually expect new discoveries when you read the Bible, or do you expect affirmation/confirmation of something you're aware of already? Why?

5. Why would anyone feel that the Bible is 'out of date'? What makes the Bible as relevant today as it was a thousand years ago?

6. In what ways do the words of scripture guide your life? How does the Bible affect your personal relationships? When has scripture inspired you to act?

Wednesday 23 September, 2009

1. How do you respond to Anne's statement that 'tithing isn't an obligation but a privilege'?

2. How does the Bible describe tithing? What examples does the Bible use to describe tithing? Given this definition/these examples, do you tithe? If not, why not?

3. If so, why do you tithe? Have you always tithed?

4. What do you consider 'the first fruits of all you produce' in your life? How does this view influence your giving?

5. Who has inspired you to be generous in your giving? How?

6. How does your church community spend the money it receives? Does your church tithe? How can you inspire your church to be more generous?

Wednesday 30 September, 2009

1. Have you ever tried journalling as part of your regular devotional time? If so, describe how you go about it and why.

2. One of the paradoxes of the Christian life is Jesus' charge to be 'wise as serpents' and 'harmless as doves'. How do you reconcile that paradox in your own life?

3. How do you typically feel towards people who 'stir up trouble' in your life? What methods have you discovered to help you let go of anger towards them and the desire to retaliate?

4. How do you cause problems for other people?

5. Who are some of the people welcomed in your community of faith? Who is not welcome? Does your church reflect the variety of people who are welcome at God's table?

6. For what reasons and in what ways do you proclaim Christ?

7. How is Christ proclaimed in your community of faith?

Wednesday 7 October, 2009

1. What does the image of the potter and the clay say about our relationship with God?

2. How do you feel about 'the concept of being clay and not having a voice in [your] development'?

3. Pots are useful. In what ways are you useful to God? To the community of faith? To other people in the world?

4. Use the image of the potter and the clay to describe the kind of person God has created you to be.

5. In what ways can you demonstrate your trust in God's plans for your life?

6. Consider the quoted scripture. When have you found yourself turning things upside down in your relationship with God?

7. Do you see yourself as a display bowl, a serving dish or an ashtray? Why do you feel this way? What could change this view or self-image?

Wednesday 14 October, 2009

1. What do you believe about prayer? How does prayer work? What is its purpose? Is it OK to pray about some things but not others? Does God hear prayers?

2. When have you asked God for what seemed impossible? Why did you think God could/would not act in this matter?

3. What does the scripture say about the community of faith? In what ways is your church community like Peter's? How is it different?

4. When praying for God to intercede in events, how specific are you?

5. Have you ever prayed for something specific, found it to occur, and then were surprised?

6. What have you prayed for constantly? What effect does 'praying constantly' have on our spiritual life?

Wednesday 21 October, 2009

1. Have you ever wondered, 'Who is my neighbour?' Did Jesus' parable answer your question? What does the scripture say about being a good neighbour?

2. When have you turned away when someone asked for your help? How did you feel?

3. In what ways do you show people God's love?

4. In what ways does the community of faith love neighbours? Who are some of the neighbours God commands the church to love?

5. Several biblical passages indicate that Christians have a variety of gifts (e.g. Rom. 12 and 1 Cor. 12). Does this mean that we need to specialise in our ministry — eschewing areas of service that don't fit specifically into our areas of talent/skill? Why or why not?

6. How would you describe 'the life God wants us to live'?

Wednesday 28 October, 2009

1. What does the story of Jonah tell us about God and God's relationship with people?

2. When have you been like Jonah? When have you wanted someone punished, and resented (just a little) God's mercy?

3. In what ways does the church turn away from God? Where in the world would God send prophets today?

4. If, as individuals and nations, we pray for our enemies, how are we changed? How is the world changed?

5. Describe an experience when you received justice and another experience when you were extended compassion. Which of the two experiences had a greater impact on your life and why?

6. Have you ever wished that God would 'exchange mercy for wrath' when an individual or a group of people faced the consequences of a crime or atrocity? How do you think God perceives this situation?

7. How easy do you find it to love your enemies? Is this the same type of love that we show for our friends and family?

8. How do your prayers for your enemies differ from those for your friends and family?

9. With which prophet do you most identify? Why?

Wednesday 4 November, 2009

1. How do you think being a 'peacekeeper' differs from being a 'peacemaker'? Are there needs for both? Why?

2. Think of a 'peacemaker' you know. How does this person demonstrate peacemaking? How can we be more deliberate about making peace in everyday situations?

3. Think of someone you know personally whom you disagree with about some issue(s). Do you tend to keep peace or make peace with this person? Why?

4. Where is one place in the world that desperately needs peace and peacemakers? How can we participate in bringing peace to places far from us?

5. In the household where you grew up, did you deal with conflict directly or try to 'sweep it under the carpet'? What did you learn from that approach? What do you see as good about the way that was not yours?

6. We sometimes equate forgiveness with reconciliation. How are they alike, and how are they different? When might reconciliation not be possible? When might it not be desirable or wise?

7. The reading for today connects peacemaking with humility and wisdom. Why would peacemaking require these qualities?

Wednesday 11 November, 2009

1. Can you think of a situation in which Jesus did not attend to calls on his time and attention? Why didn't he? What can we learn from this?

2. Think about the writer's statement, 'The interruptions in our lives may be God calling us to serve.' Do you agree or disagree with the writer and why?

3. Think of a relationship important to you that began through an unplanned encounter or by accident. Looking back, how do you see God working in your life through this relationship? What has the relationship brought to you that you would not have wanted to miss?

4. How do you usually respond to interruptions when you are doing something that you feel is important? Do you think your usual manner reflects Christian values?

5. Read again the story of Bartimaeus. What about Bartimaeus in this story surprises or impresses you? What about Jesus surprises or impresses you?

6. How do you listen to others? To whom do you have trouble listening, and why? What does this meditation suggest that you might do to show God's concern to this person?

Wednesday 18 November, 2009

1. What is the difference between a talent and a skill? Does God give both? Do we tend to value one more than the other? Should we?

2. What talent that you don't have would you really like to have? Why? How would or could you use this talent for God if you had it?

3. What is the most unusual talent you have seen being used for God? How was it being used?

4. What are some characteristics that many of your family members share? If you share it, how do you feel about that? If you don't share it, how do you feel about that? What are some 'family characteristics' that we should all share in God's family?

5. What is your earliest image of God? What do you think shaped this image (e.g. wishful thinking, etc.)? Is that image still a part of how you see God? Why or why not?

6. What things do you have trouble understanding about God?

7. What are your three favourite images of God from the Bible? What does each of these images say to you about God's nature?

Wednesday 25 November, 2009

1. Do you agree that God's directions about following Christ are clear? If so, in what ways? If not, in what situations do you think people need more guidance than this writer offers?

2. Think about the last time you were lost. What feelings did the experience give rise to?

3. What might the experience of being physically lost teach us about being spiritually lost?

4. Name a friend who has guided you out of a difficult situation. What 'directions' did that friend give to help you find your way?

5. About what situations in life do you wish the Bible gave clearer directions? About which ones do you wish the Bible were a little less clear?

6. What passages in the Bible are not meant as literal directions for our lives today? For example, do you think we should stone people to death publicly for some offences (Lev. 24:16; Deut. 21:18-21, etc.)? Should women be barred from speaking out in church (1 Tim. 2:11-12; 1 Cor. 14:33-35)? Should people whose children are in trouble be barred from leadership positions in the church (Tit. 1:6; 1 Tim. 3:4-5, 12)? Why are these passages in the Bible if we are not meant to live by them exactly as they appear?

Wednesday 2 December, 2009

1. What news items from this week have been disturbing to you? What do you think God wants you to do about your feelings? About the specific situations that caused them?

2. What signs of hope have you seen around you in the past week? Why do these give you hope?

3. Does the Bible promise God's people happiness? If not, what does the Bible offer in its place?

4. Think back to a difficult time in your life. Were you able to be hopeful? What characteristics of God help you to be hopeful even in difficult situations?

5. Researchers say that some attitudes and behaviour, such as worry, optimism, distrust, impulsiveness, recklessness, even a tendency toward violence, are inborn, that these may be 'default' settings for some of us. How do Bible passages such as 'rejoice always' or 'trust in the Lord' apply to such people? How do you think a person who finds it difficult to feel hopeful might respond to admonitions to 'trust in God and do not doubt'?

6. How much control do we have over how we feel? Can we change our feelings? If so, by what means? Does the Bible tell us to feel any particular way about anything? Or does the Bible deal more with behaviour than feelings?

Wednesday 9 December, 2009

1. What does 'pure and genuine religion' mean to you? What do you think the writer might be saying in a broader sense about our responsibility for people around us?

2. Describe a command of God in scripture that you freely and easily support in theory but have great difficulty following in practice. Why do you find it so difficult?

3. When have you seen or heard of someone showing the sort of kindness and generosity that this minister showed?

4. How do people learn to be generous? How does this minister's behaviour reflect God's nature?

5. What negative images do we have of parents whose children are in foster care? Of the children themselves? How does this meditation challenge such ideas?

6. How do you think God sees foster children and their parents? What does God want for them? How can we be a part of God's working in their lives?

7. Do you agree with this writer's statement that we are all orphans until we come to God? Are all humans God's children, or does that label apply only to those who have come to faith? Why do you say this?

8. When have you seen God's power dramatically change someone's life? How has God changed you and your life?

Wednesday 16 December, 2009

1. Describe what makes a person respectable. How does a respectable person differ from anyone else? Why is reputation important? How and why is being a Christian more than being respectable?

2. Do you think there are some places where God is not present? Do you think God exists in places or in people?

3. For what beauty are you often thankful? How can we make encounters with beauty into reminders to pray? What strategies can we use to help us remember to express thanks to God?

4. How are believers present in your community in places like the one this writer describes? How is your church involved in these ministries? If it is not, why not?

5. Read aloud slowly the day's suggested scripture reading. What part of the passage tugs at you or especially gets your attention? Why does this affect you? What action does it suggest that you might take?

6. When was the last time you did something for someone who was hungry or a stranger or in need of clothes or sick or imprisoned (Matt 25:34-37)? Which of these groups of people do you feel most comfortable serving? With which are you least comfortable? Why? How do you experience Christ's presence as you serve others?

Wednesday 23 December, 2009

1. Describe how you sense or know you are God's child. Have you always sensed this, or did something happen to make you feel God's love?

2. What do you think the 'gift of life' would be like without life eternal? What does God offer us for hope?

3. Can you recall a particular time when the scriptures first 'became real' to you? Or is this an ongoing process?

4. When have you been close to someone dealing with a terminal illness, as this writer is? Was the person able to speak openly about the situation? What can we learn from such situations?

5. The apostle John recorded, 'There is no fear in love, but perfect love casts out fear' (1 Jn. 4:18). When has fear kept you from feeling loved by a family member or friend? By God? What was the source of this fear? Have you overcome it? How?

6. This writer's experience of growing up feeling unloved seems common. How might such an experience affect someone's behaviour? How might it affect their feelings about God?

7. Was affection expressed openly in the household where you grew up? Did you and those around you say 'I love you'? How have attitudes about expressing affection changed during your lifetime? Do you think these changes are for the good?

Wednesday 30 December, 2009

1. What new possibilities and desires do you long for in your life? What changes in your life are needed to make you a 'new creation' (2 Cor. 5:17)? What prevents you from seeking/realising these changes?

2. When you think of doing what Patricia did, what thoughts and feelings come to mind? Would you be able to do what she did? Why or why not?

3. If you felt that God wanted you to give up all your possessions, what would you have most difficulty parting with? Which two or three things might you want to bargain about keeping?

4. Have you ever experienced a time when you felt as if you had begun over again — that many of the familiar things in your life had changed? If so, describe that time. What effect did this have on you?

5. Recount a time when you had to change. How did you respond? What was the result? Where do you see God in this process?

6. Do you sense that God is calling you to let go of something familiar? What is it? What 'new thing' do you think God desires for you? How are you co-operating with God in it? Where are you resisting, and why?

7. What new thing is God doing in your community? In your community of faith? How are you a part of both? How might you be more involved in them?

Bible Reading Resources Pack

A pack of resources and ideas to help to promote Bible reading in your church is available from BRF. The pack, which will be of use at any time during the year (but especially for Bible Sunday in October), includes sample readings from BRF's Bible reading notes and The People's Bible Commentary, a sermon outline, an all-age sketch, a children's activity, information about BRF's ministry and much more.

Unless you specify the month in which you would like the pack sent, we will send it immediately on receipt of your order. We greatly appreciate your donations towards the cost of producing the pack (without them we would not be able to make the pack available) and we welcome your comments about the contents of the pack and your ideas for future ones.

This coupon should be sent to:
BRF, 15 The Chambers, Vineyard, Abingdon OX14 3FE

Name ....

Address ....

.... Postcode ....

Telephone ....

Email ....

Please send me .... Bible Reading Resources Pack(s)

Please send the pack now/ in .... (month).

I enclose a donation for £ .... towards the cost of the pack.

BRF is a Registered Charity

UR0709

Subscriptions

From January 2010, The Upper Room will be published in January, May and September.

Individual subscriptions
The subscription rate for orders for 4 or fewer copies includes postage and packing: THE UPPER ROOM annual individual subscription   £13.50

Church subscriptions
Orders for 5 copies or more, sent to ONE address, are post free:
THE UPPER ROOM annual church subscription   £10.50

Please do not send payment with order for a church subscription. We will send an invoice with your first order.

Please note that the annual billing period for Church Subscriptions runs from 1 May to 30 April.

Copies of the notes may also be obtained from Christian bookshops.

From January 2010 single copies of The Upper Room will cost £3.50. Prices valid until 30 April 2011.

Individual Subscriptions

☐ Please send me a Bible reading resources pack to encourage Bible reading in my church

☐ I would like to take out a subscription myself (complete your name and address details only once)

☐ I would like to give a gift subscription (please complete both name and address sections below)

Your name ....

Your address ....

.... Postcode ....

Gift subscription name ....

Gift subscription address ....

.... Postcode ....

Gift message (20 words max.) ....

....

Please send *The Upper Room* beginning with the January / May / September 2010 issue: (delete as applicable)

THE UPPER ROOM ☐ £13.50

Please complete the payment details below and send, with appropriate payment, to: BRF, 15 The Chambers, Vineyard, Abingdon OX14 3FE.

Total enclosed £ .... (cheques should be made payable to 'BRF')

Payment by cheque ☐ postal order ☐ Visa ☐ Mastercard ☐ Switch ☐

Card no: ☐☐☐☐☐☐☐☐☐☐☐☐☐☐☐☐☐☐☐

Expires: ☐☐☐☐ Security code: ☐☐☐☐

Issue no (Switch): ☐☐☐☐

Signature (essential if paying by credit/Switch card) ....

☐ Please do not send me further information about BRF publications.

BRF is a Registered Charity

UR0709

Church Subscriptions

☐ Please send me a Bible reading resources pack to encourage Bible reading in my church

Please send me .... copies of *The Upper Room* January / May / September 2010 issue: (delete as applicable)

Name ....

Address ....

....

Postcode ....

Telephone ....

Email ....

Please send this completed form to:
BRF, 15 The Chambers, Vineyard, Abingdon OX14 3FE.

Please do not send payment with this order. We will send an invoice with your first order.

Christian bookshops: All good Christian bookshops stock BRF publications. For your nearest stockist, please contact BRF.
Telephone: The BRF office is open between 09.15 and 17.30. To place your order, phone 01865 319700; fax 01865 319701.
Web: Visit www.brf.org.uk

BRF is a Registered Charity